50 Walks in
DURHAM &
NORTHUMBERLAND

First published 2003
Researched and written by John Gillham, Dennis Kelsall, Anthony Toole and David
Winpenny. Introduction by Chris Bagshaw

Produced by AA Publishing
© Automobile Association Developments Limited 2003
Illustrations © Automobile Association Developments Limited 2003
Reprinted 2004

Published by AA Publishing (a trading name of Automobile Association Developments
Limited, whose registered office is Millstream, Maidenhead, Windsor, SL4 5GD; registered
number 1878835)

o|s Ordnance This product includes mapping data licensed from Ordnance Survey®
Survey® with the permission of the Controller of Her Majesty's Stationery Office.
© Crown copyright 2004. All rights reserved. Licence number 399221

ISBN 0 7495 3623 3

A02038

Visit the AA Publishing website at www.theAA.com
Paste-up and editorial by Outcrop Publishing Services Ltd, Cumbria for AA Publishing
Printed in Italy by G Canale & C SPA, Torino, Italy

Legend

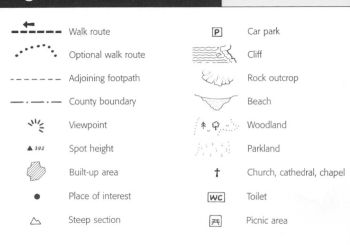

◄━━━━━	Walk route	P	Car park
••••••	Optional walk route	≈≈≈≈	Cliff
━━━━━━	Adjoining footpath		Rock outcrop
━ ∙ ━ ∙ ━	County boundary		Beach
☼	Viewpoint	♠ ♣	Woodland
▲ 392	Spot height		Parkland
	Built-up area	†	Church, cathedral, chapel
●	Place of interest	WC	Toilet
△	Steep section	舟	Picnic area

Durham & Northumberland locator map

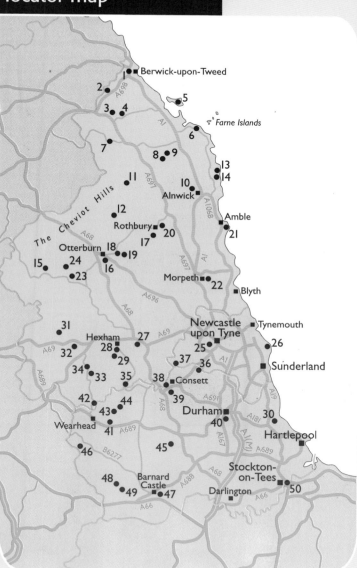

Berwick-upon-Tweed
2
1
3 4
5
Farne Islands
6
7
8 9
11
13
14
10
Alnwick
12
Amble
Rothbury
20
21
17
The Cheviot Hills
Otterburn 18
19
15
24 16
23
Morpeth
22
Blyth
31
Newcastle upon Tyne
Tynemouth
Hexham
27
A69
32
28
25
26
34
29
37
Sunderland
33 35
36
42
38
Consett
30
44
39
43
Durham
Hartlepool
Wearhead
41
40
46
45
Stockton-on-Tees
48
Barnard Castle
50
49
47
Darlington

Contents

Contents

WALK	**RATING**	**DISTANCE**	**PAGE**

Rating: Each walk is rated for its relative difficulty compared to the other walks in this book. Walks marked 🚶🚶 🚶 🚶 are likely to be shorter and easier with little total ascent. The hardest walks are marked 🚶🚶 🚶🚶 🚶🚶 .

Walking in Safety: For advice and safety tips ➤ 128.

Introducing Durham & Northumberland

The north east of England means many things to many different people. For some it is the bawdy charm of Newcastle's Bigg Market, the aspirant artiness of Gateshead's new Baltic – the Centre for Contemporary Art or the Angel of the North. For others it is the medieval splendour of Durham's fine cathedral, the towering remains of Northumberland's great castles, or the breathtaking ambition of Hadrian's Wall. Of course it is all these things and many more besides. From the remote Cheviots with their winter caps of snow, to the grouse moors of Durham and the high Pennines, this is a huge space filled with history and wildlife and the stories of people working and at war.

In its south east corner, bold Middlesbrough has a new riverside frontage, the remarkable transporter bridge its centrepiece. Upriver, the Tees shimmies its way into the hill country of the North Pennines, passing castles and abbeys before ending on the slopes of Cross Fell and the Cumbrian border. This block of upland stretches away to the Tyne Gap in the north and incorporates some of England's most remote communities. This was once mining country and the remains of lead workings dominate the landscape. In Weardale and Allendale, industrial villages huddle in the valley floor. No one mines here now and, aside from the occasional quarry, the only interruption breaking the still mountain air is the cry of a grouse or a pheasant, rising up from the shooting estates which now control much of the countryside. Further east, the steep-sided valleys proved challenging to the industrialists who wanted to rip out the county's coal reserves. Now they, and their iron-founding collaborators, have vanished, leaving a legacy of beautifully engineered railway lines and bridges for the walker to discover.

Much has been written about Durham itself, the great cathedral standing high on a bend in the River Wear. More, perhaps, will be written in the future of East Durham's fine coast, lately emerged from the coat of black coal waste which had clothed it for over 100 years.

The North Pennines come to an end at the Tyne Gap and here, down the valley of the Tyne, the Emperor Hadrian built his great wall, to defend 'civilised' Roman Britain from the hordes that populated the north. Now a World Heritage Site, there are several sections of this remarkable 2,000-year-old structure where you

PUBLIC TRANSPORT ⓘ

Like many parts of Britain, transport in the north east of England is excellent in the urban areas and patchy and less reliable in the remoter rural districts. There is a considerable amount of money being invested in coordinating buses and trains, making through connections possible from Berwick all the way to Middlesbrough. Traveline is the best place to start planning itineraries and connections, call 0870 608 2 608 or visit the North of England section at jplanner.org.uk.

can patrol its ramparts as the legionaries might have done. At its eastern end you can discover the home of Bede, England's first historian, and see the communities that gave rise to the Jarrow marchers 1,500 years later. Close by is the city of Newcastle, its distinctive bridges spanning the Tyne to the neighbouring borough of Gateshead.

North of here the English coast stretches to the border town of Berwick-upon-Tweed. The hinterland, rising to the grassy heights of the Cheviots, begins in the dunes and fertile plain, before crinkling through moorland and pasture dotted by castles and tower houses. Much of the area to the west is forested, with woodland stretching over the borders into Scotland and Cumbria. This is the land of the Reivers, lawless families who once thrived here.

It has been hard to capture the spirit of Durham and Northumberland in just 50 walks, but we hope you'll find this selection a worthy taster to this fine region.

Using this Book

Information panels

An information panel for each walk shows its relative difficulty (➤ 5), the distance and total amount of ascent. An indication of the gradients you will encounter is shown by the rating ▲ ▲ ▲ (no steep slopes) to ▲ ▲ ▲ (several very steep slopes).

Maps

There are 30 maps, covering 40 of the walks. Some walks have a suggested option in the same area. The information panel for these walks will tell you how much extra walking is involved. On short-cut suggestions the panel will tell you the total distance if you set out from the start of the main walk. Where an option returns to the same point on the main walk, just the distance of the loop is given. Where an option leaves the main walk at one point and returns to it at another, then the distance shown is for the whole walk. The minimum time suggested is for reasonably fit walkers and doesn't allow for stops. Each walk has a suggested map. Laminated aqua3 maps are longer lasting and water resistant.

Start Points

The start of each walk is given as a six-figure grid reference prefixed by two letters indicating which 100km square of the National Grid it refers to. You'll find more information on grid references on most Ordnance Survey maps.

Dogs

We have tried to give dog owners useful advice about how dog friendly each walk is. Please respect other countryside users. Keep your dog under control, especially around livestock, and obey local bylaws and other dog control notices.

Car Parking

Many of the car parks suggested are public, but occasionally you may find you have to park on the roadside or in a lay-by. Please be considerate when you leave your car, ensuring that access roads or gates are not blocked and that other vehicles can pass safely. Remember that pub car parks are private and should not be used unless you have the owner's permission.

Walk 1

Berwick Town Walls

Explore old Berwick and then take a longer ramble beside the Tweed.

•DISTANCE•	6½ miles (10.4km)
•MINIMUM TIME•	2hrs 15min
•ASCENT / GRADIENT•	Negligible
•LEVEL OF DIFFICULTY•	
•PATHS•	Paved pathways and field paths, flood-meadows may be wet and muddy, particularly around high tide, 4 stiles
•LANDSCAPE•	Town, riverside and woodland
•SUGGESTED MAP•	aqua3 OS Explorer 346 Berwick-upon-Tweed
•START / FINISH•	Grid reference: NT 998529
•DOG FRIENDLINESS•	On leads in town and near livestock
•PARKING•	Below ramparts outside Scots Gate
•PUBLIC TOILETS•	At car park, below ramparts
•NOTE•	Sheer, unguarded drop from outer edge of town walls and bastions, keep to marked pathways
•CONTRIBUTOR•	Dennis Kelsall

BACKGROUND TO THE WALK

Overlooking the Tweed Estuary, Berwick is a true Border town and, despite it standing on the northern bank, it is actually in England. Yet in the 12th century it was a Scottish Royal Burgh and the country's most prosperous port, busy with the export of grain from a richly fertile hinterland. The town first fell into English hands in 1174 but, for the next 300 years, was repeatedly attacked by one side or the other as each tried to wrest control. It changed ownership so many times that the long-suffering inhabitants must have wondered just whose side they were on.

An English Fortress
When the political shuttlecock finally came to rest in 1482, Berwick found itself in England, although it retained the status of an independent state until 1836. However, the Scottish threat remained and, cut off from the surrounding countryside that had once made it rich, prosperity continued to be elusive until renewed threats of the 'Auld Alliance' prompted Elizabeth I to commission new fortifications in 1557. Wiping away much of the town's medieval walls, no longer effective against modern artillery, she spent £128,000 to enclose the town within thick ramparts and complex projecting bastions, from which defensive artillery could rake attacking forces. With hindsight, she probably wasted her money, for the expected attack never came and the economic boost to the town was short-lived.

A Developing Town
It was not until the succession of James VI of Scotland to the English throne in 1603 that the town embarked on its road to recovery. The graceful bridge was built and the harbour developed and, by the middle of the 18th century, there was a regular packet service to London carrying both passengers and cargo. For the first time the salmon, for which the Tweed is still renowned, appeared in the capital's markets, kept fresh during the voyage by

ice produced on the quayside. The boom continued into the 19th century, with a spate of elegant building catering for the civil, military, religious and domestic needs of the town.

Perversely, the spanner that brought the economic wheel to a halt was the very thing that might have been envisaged to do just the opposite – the arrival of the railway. Whilst it opened up many new areas and industries by providing cheap, fast and convenient transport for freight and people, it did no good at all for the coastal seafaring trade. The port, previously the key to the town's success, gradually dwindled and with it, the trade it had once brought. Despite that, Berwick continues as a busy and attractive market town, with much of interest to see as you wander around its Elizabethan defences, unique for their completeness.

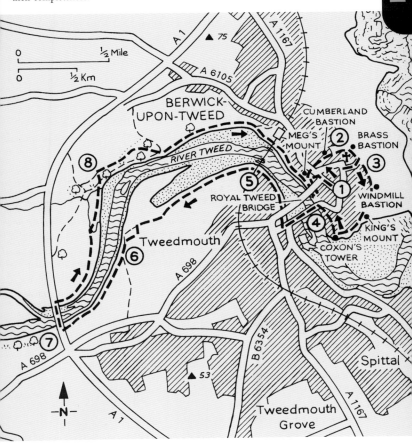

Walk 1 Directions

① From the old Town Hall, walk west along **Marygate** to **Scots Gate**. Immediately before it, turn left to find a gateway on the right, where you can climb on to the walls by

Meg's Mount. Follow the wall back over Scots Gate and on past the **Cumberland Bastion**.

② The next battery, **Brass Bastion**, lies at the northern corner of the town. Some 100yds (91m) beyond, a path descends inside the wall to

Walk 1

meet **The Parade** by the corner of the parish church graveyard. Turn right past the barracks to the church, both of which are well worth visiting.

③ Return to the walls and continue around, passing **Windmill Bastion** and the site of the earlier Edward VI fort. Beyond **King's Mount**, the walls rise above the Tweed Estuary before turning upriver at **Coxon's Tower**, past elegant Georgian terraces and on above the old quay.

④ Leave the walls at **Bridge End** and cross the **Old Bridge**. Turn right past the war memorial, go beneath the modern **Royal Tweed Bridge** and remain by the river beyond, shortly passing below Stephenson's railway viaduct.

⑤ The way continues upstream along an often muddy path. Where the bank widens to a rough meadow, keep along the left side to a kissing gate in the far corner and carry on at the edge of the next field. Eventually, beyond a gate, a contained path skirts a water treatment plant. Turning left through a second gate, it emerges on to a tarmac track, where you should turn right.

⑥ At a bend 40yds (37m) on, bear off right along a field edge above the steep river bank. Continue in the next field but, towards its far end, look for a stepped path descending the bank to a stream. Rising to a stile beyond, bear right to the main road.

⑦ Cross the Tweed and drop right on to a path, signed 'Berwick via Plantation', which crosses a couple of stiles to a riverside pasture. Walk away beside the left boundary for about ½ mile (800m). After crossing the head of a stream, move away from the hedge, aiming to meet the river below a wooded bank. Over a side bridge, bear right to a stile and continue through the trees beyond to a path at the top of the bank.

⑧ Go right, eventually dropping from the wood by a cottage, where a riverside promenade leads back to Berwick. Just beyond the **Royal Tweed Bridge**, turn sharp left, climbing back beneath it and continue beside the town walls to return to **Meg's Mount**.

Norham and the Tweed Valley

A delightful wander along the Tweed, returning past Norham's former railway station and ancient castle.

•DISTANCE•	4½ miles (7.2km)
•MINIMUM TIME•	1hr 30min
•ASCENT / GRADIENT•	205ft (62m)
•LEVEL OF DIFFICULTY•	
•PATHS•	Field and woodland paths, 4 stiles
•LANDSCAPE•	Undulating river valley, agricultural land and woods
•SUGGESTED MAP•	aqua3 OS Explorer 339 Kelso & Coldstream
•START / FINISH•	Grid reference: NT 899473
•DOG FRIENDLINESS•	On lead near livestock
•PARKING•	Roadside parking in Norham
•PUBLIC TOILETS•	Close to village centre
•CONTRIBUTOR•	Dennis Kelsall

BACKGROUND TO THE WALK

Walking through the spacious streets of Norham, where low cottages and splendid mini-town houses lead to an open green graced by a cross that has stood there for centuries, it is hard to believe that this was once the most dangerous place in all England, or so we are told in Sir Walter Scott's epic poem *Marmion*. Yet, he was probably right, for when the bold knight, Sir William Marmion, actually came to Norham in 1319, it was indeed a troubled place, a state that had existed since the Norman Conquest in 1066 and was to continue into the 16th century.

The Prince Bishops

Once William I established himself in England, he assumed the country would buckle down to Norman order, but the north was not so inclined. A series of revolts incited William to embark upon a campaign of death and wholesale destruction that became known as the 'Harrying of the North'. However, even that was only effective in the short term and he delegated the job of governing these unruly people to the Bishops of Durham. Dubbed the Prince Bishops they became very powerful and, in effect, ruled Northumbria as kings. However, the trouble didn't stop there, because the Scots had always regarded the land as theirs anyway, and for centuries the North was repeatedly devastated, either by battle or from the passage of one warring faction or the other, plundering food and just about anything else of any use as they passed through.

The Castle

Norham's castle was founded by Bishop Ranulph Flambard in 1121 as a defence against the Scots. Yet, in spite of a formidable situation on high cliffs above the Tweed, they still managed to take the castle twice during the next 16 years. Under the control of the bishops, the fortress was rebuilt and extended from 1157 into the 13th century, with such effect that it withstood a 40-day siege in 1215. A century of peace followed, but with the return of hostilities, Norham was again in the front line. During the next 200 years, it was besieged six times and captured twice, the last occasion being in 1513 as the confident Scots made their fateful journey towards Flodden. Afterwards, the English undertook extensive repairs to strengthen the defences against the modern artillery that had been its downfall. However, the political wind changed and the castle passed to the Crown in 1559, after Bishop Tunstall refused to take the Oath of Supremacy. No longer required as a strategic outpost, it gradually declined to the spectacular ruin that it is today.

Ancient Settlers and Victorian Visitors

Recent archaeological work suggests that the area was probably first fortified during the early Iron Age. The high embankment towering above the field path, leading towards the castle near the end of the walk, is believed to be part of an earthen rampart defending the eastern aspect of the headland above the village. Traces of a third outer medieval bailey and more recent artillery emplacements were also found, indicating a much larger fortified enclosure than was previously considered. The field path to the castle is thought to have been created after Norham Station opened, to provide a ready access for Victorian visitors, eager to realise the romantic dreams inspired by Scott's poem and Turner's painting of the castle.

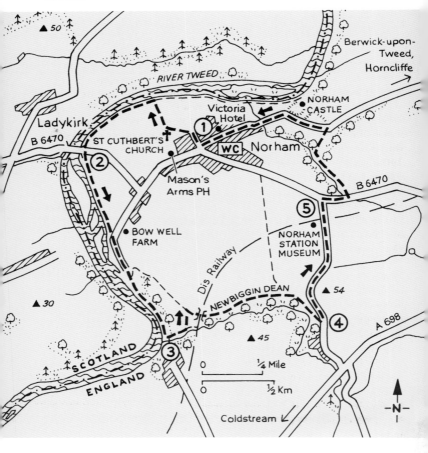

Walk 2 Directions

① Leave the village green by the cross, heading along **Pedwell Way** to **St Cuthbert's Church**. In the churchyard, walk along a grassy path between the graves to pass behind the north side of the church, where you will find a stile marking the head of an enclosed path down to the **Tweed**. Follow the river bank upstream, shortly arriving at **Ladykirk** and **Norham Bridge**.

> ### *WHERE TO EAT AND DRINK* ⓘ
> You've got a choice in Norham as the village is blessed with two inviting pubs, the **Victoria Hotel** and the **Mason's Arms**. Both serve appetising food in an attractive setting and offer children's menus for the younger members of your party.

② Immediately beyond, go over a ladder stile on the left, turn right and continue at the field edge. Towards its far end, approaching **Bow Well Farm**, look for a stile which takes the path down a tree-clad bank and out to a lane. Walk right and, at the end, pass through a gate, signed 'Twizell Bridge', to carry on across a pasture in front of a cottage and then through a second gate into a wood. An undulating path continues above the river.

③ When you reach a path junction by a footbridge, go left through a broken gate. Bear left again a little further on and climb to another junction at the top of the wood. Now turn right to walk above **Newbiggin Dean**, passing beneath the stone arch of a railway viaduct. Shortly, at a fork beyond a stile, take the right branch, signed 'East Biggin', which eventually leads out on to a lane.

④ Turn left, climbing over a hill to descend between the piers of a dismantled railway bridge. Just before here, to the left, is the former **Norham Station**, which closed in 1964. Its buildings are now restored and house a railway museum. Continue to walk on to the end of the lane.

> ### *WHILE YOU'RE THERE* ⓘ
> Drive to nearby Horncliffe, where the **Honey Farm** contains a fascinating exhibition explaining the complex society within a beehive and how the best honey is produced. Just beyond the farm is **Union Chain Bridge**, one of the engineering marvels of its day. When built, it was the longest wrought iron suspension bridge in the western world, a record held until Telford's Menai Bridge opened five years later in 1826.

⑤ Turn right, but then leave some 250yds (229m) further on, through an opening on the left, signed as a bridleway to Norham Castle. Keep ahead along the field edge to the bottom corner, where a gated track continues beside a brook through trees. Shortly, go left over a bridge into a field, and there turn right, following its edge out to a lane. Turn left and walk past the entrance of **Norham Castle**, eventually returning to the village.

> ### *WHAT TO LOOK FOR* ⓘ
> Pop into **St Cuthbert's Church** (you'll pass it on the first part of the walk), whose tradition goes back to the days of the Celtic saints, when St Aiden crossed the Tweed here on his way to Lindisfarne in AD 635. The first stone church was founded in 830, but the present building dates from around the same time as the medieval castle. Look for the effigy of a 13th-century knight, discovered buried near the side altar during restoration works in 1883.

Etal and Ford

Discover the rolling countryside between these very different estate villages.

•DISTANCE•	6 miles (9.7km)
•MINIMUM TIME•	2hrs
•ASCENT / GRADIENT•	525ft (160m) ▲▲▲
•LEVEL OF DIFFICULTY•	🚶 🚶 🚶
•PATHS•	Lanes, tracks and field paths, 2 stiles on Walk 4
•LANDSCAPE•	Undulating farmland broken by small woods and copses
•SUGGESTED MAP•	aqua3 OS Explorer 339 Kelso & Coldstream
•START / FINISH•	Grid reference: NT 925392
•DOG FRIENDLINESS•	Mostly on lead; grazing land and game coverts
•PARKING•	Free car park by Etal Castle
•PUBLIC TOILETS•	At Etal Castle, Ford Forge and in Ford village
•CONTRIBUTOR•	Dennis Kelsall

BACKGROUND TO THE WALK

Although Etal and Ford are peacefully united under the ownership of the Joiceys, history reveals a bitter feud between the two families that originally held them. With the establishment of Norman rule in the North, the manors of Etal and Ford were granted sometime in the 12th century to the Manners and the Herons respectively. It seems that conflict arose out of a power struggle between them, which finally came to a head in 1428, when William Ford was killed in an affray at Etal Castle. His widow accused John Manners of maliciously killing her husband and, although John subsequently forked out a hefty compensation, the feud rumbled on for another ten years.

Border Troubles

The first manors would have been little more than stout wooden structures, surrounded by palisades as defence against intruders, with stone buildings appearing later only as means allowed. The Herons were the first to be granted a licence to crenellate, in 1341, and the Manners soon followed, building up their existing hall into the tower house that still stands at Etal's north western corner, and adding the enclosing walls and gatehouse a little later. The two castles suffered many attacks from marauding bands, with Ford being largely destroyed in 1385. But it was not until 1513 that real trouble arrived, when a force of 30,000 Scots appeared with James IV at its head, after taking the castles at both Norham and Wark. The defence at Etal collapsed after a brief bombardment and the capitulation of Ford quickly followed. Yet, for whatever reason, James seems not to have pressed home his advantage, for he lingered a few days at Ford allowing the Earl of Surrey vital time to bring an army north. They met days later at Flodden and, although heavily outnumbered, the English routed the Scots, killing James along with many of his nobles. Etal, now back in English hands, was used to store the captured Scottish artillery that James had hauled south with his army.

As the century progressed, the area settled down and the need for stark fortifications became a thing of the past. Etal deteriorated and was finally abandoned as a home, the Carrs, its then owners, building a mansion to the east of the village in 1748, whilst Ford was remodelled shortly after as a grand country house. The two villages have developed very different characters, Ford portraying the best of early 19th-century town planning, whilst Etal gives the impression of a romantic pastoral age. Yet these pretty cottages are in fact newer than those at Ford. Although remodelled when the Carrs built their grand house, by the late 19th century, Etal's quaint thatched cottages had become totally insanitary and when Lord Joicey bought the estate in 1908, he had them completely rebuilt.

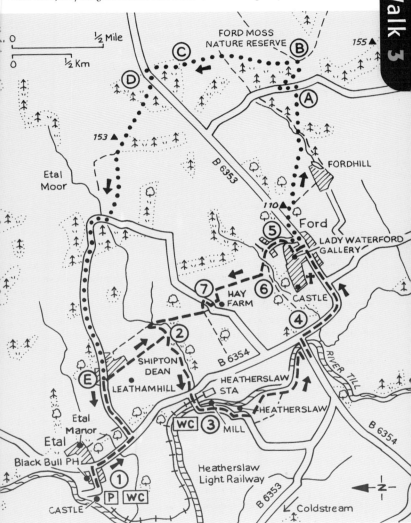

Walk 3 Directions

① Walk through the village of Etal to the main road and turn right towards Ford, shortly leaving along a lane on the left-hand side to **Leathamhill**. When you reach the cottages, go right on a track beside the sawmill, signed 'Heatherslaw and Hay Farm', and keep on across the fields beyond.

Walk 3

② At the bottom, by **Shipton Dean**, go through a gate on the right into a strip of wood. Beyond, head down the edge of successive fields to regain the main road opposite **Heatherslaw Station**. Cross to the lane opposite, following it over a bridge and around past **Heatherslaw Mill**.

③ Keep going to **Heatherslaw farm** but, after the right-hand bend, leave through a five-bar gate on the left, signed 'Ford Bridge'. Pass a shed and go through a second gate. Bear right, crossing to another gate in the far corner of the field by the river. Continue above the **Till** to **Ford Bridge**, there following the field edge away from the river to a gate leading out to a lane. Head back along it, crossing the bridge to a junction.

④ To the right, the road winds up to Ford. Go past the entrance to the church and **Ford Castle** before turning left into the village. At the bottom, opposite the **Lady Waterford Gallery**, turn right to ascend to a junction opposite **Jubilee Cottage**.

⑤ Now go left but, where the lane later bends sharply right beyond the former stables, leave through a gate on the left into a wood, signed 'Hay Farm'. Ignore the obvious track ahead and, instead, bear left on a path through the trees to a stream.

Continue over a bridge to emerge in a field and follow its perimeter to the left above the wood.

⑥ Instead of going through the corner gate, turn right up the field edge to the top of the hill. There, pass left through a gate and cross a small field to a track in front of **Hay Farm cottages**.

WHILE YOU'RE THERE ⓘ

Take a ride on the **Heatherslaw Light Railway**, a 15-inch gauge steam railway running between Heatherslaw Mill and Etal Castle. The line opened in July 1989 and, for much of its length, runs beside the River Till, which is rich in wildlife. The train's passing appears not to disturb it, and there is often a good chance of seeing some of the more elusive species, such as a kingfisher or even an otter.

---

⑦ Walk as far as another track on the right, which leads past barns to a junction. Turn right to enter a gate 20yds (18m) along on the left, signed 'Heatherslaw and Leathamhill'. Follow the field edge to a power cable post and then go right, following the boundary down and eventually passing a wood to reach the bottom corner. Drop through a gate into the trees to a bridge over a stream. Through a second gate, turn left along the field edge to return to Point ②. Retrace your outward steps to **Etal**.

WHERE TO EAT AND DRINK ⓘ

The **Black Bull** in Etal is the only thatched pub in the county and serves coffee and a good selection of bar meals. If you get stomach pangs on the way round, call in at the **Granary Café** at Heatherslaw Mill. You'll also find teas served from a **cottage** opposite the Lady Waterford Gallery in Ford.

WHAT TO LOOK FOR ⓘ

Pop into the superbly restored **Heatherslaw Mill** as you pass. There has been a watermill here on the river since the 13th century, but the present structure, built as a corn mill, is only around 150 years old. It incorporated a kiln for drying the grain as well as a store. The original machinery produces stoneground flour, used to make a range of delicious cakes and biscuits.

Ford Moss Nature Reserve

A fascinating nature reserve, occupying a moss beside old mine workings.
See map and information panel for Walk 3

•DISTANCE•	9 miles (14.5km)
•MINIMUM TIME•	3hrs
•ASCENT / GRADIENT•	750ft (229m)
•LEVEL OF DIFFICULTY•	

Walk 4 Directions (Walk 3 option)

Follow Walk 3 to Point ⑤. Go right to the main road and then left to a lay-by at the crest of the hill. Cross a stile, signed 'Fordhill', take a track into a wood and almost immediately turn left at a waymark on to a narrower path. Emerging over a wall at the top, continue along a contained walkway into the corner of an open field. Go diagonally downhill, crossing a grown-out hedge in the field middle to find a gate in the far bottom corner. In the next field, follow the right-hand boundary for 150yds (137m), leaving through a gap down to a crossing track.

Go through the gateway opposite and head on a left diagonal across the fields, eventually reaching a lane at the top, Point Ⓐ. Go left for 200yds (183m) and then sharp right on a climbing track beside a pine forest, signed 'South Moor'. Keep ahead past a gate, shortly emerging in a clearing overlooking the **Ford Moss Nature Reserve**, Point Ⓑ.

A large, shallow, waterlogged depression, Ford Moss has evolved from the accumulation of decaying vegetation over a period of 5,000 years. The process produces an ever-deepening layer of peat and, in places, the bog floats upon the underlying water.

To the left, a track leads through a gate. Just beyond, bear left again, to continue beside a perimeter wall at the edge of rough pasture. Where the wall later curves left and the ground falls away, bear right. Beyond a track, keep ahead, joining a fence over to the right, which leads past a pond to a gate, Point Ⓒ. Carry on through a copse beside the right-hand boundary, then move to the left corner, to two gates. Through the right-hand one, a path winds into forest, crossing a stream before gently climbing to emerge on to the **B6353** at Point Ⓓ.

Walk left and then go right on a forest road, signed 'Slainsfield'. Beyond the trees, continue between fields and, where the track eventually turns right, keep ahead over the crest of the hill to a gate. Now in a rough pasture, walk down beside the fence. Partway along, at a dog-leg, pass through a gate to continue on the other side, eventually emerging at the bottom on to a lane. Walk along the lane to the right, back to **Leathamhill**, rejoining Walk 3 at Point Ⓔ.

Walk 5

Lindisfarne

Explore the beginnings of Celtic Christianity and a National Nature Reserve.

•DISTANCE•	5½ miles (8.8km)
•MINIMUM TIME•	1hr 45min
•ASCENT / GRADIENT•	100ft (30m)
•LEVEL OF DIFFICULTY•	
•PATHS•	Shore and dunes, some easy scrambles (avoidable), 1 stile
•LANDSCAPE•	Dunes and expansive inter-tidal sands
•SUGGESTED MAP•	aqua3 OS Explorer 340 Holy Island & Bamburgh
•START / FINISH•	Grid reference: NU 125424
•DOG FRIENDLINESS•	Dogs should remain on leads through village
•PARKING•	Large pay-and-display car park at entrance to village
•PUBLIC TOILETS•	Signed within village
•NOTE•	Check tides; best undertaken at low tide as coastal section and causeway to island impassable at high water
•CONTRIBUTOR•	Dennis Kelsall

Walk 5 Directions

St Aiden travelled to Lindisfarne from Iona in AD 635 at the invitation of King Oswald, to bring Christianity to a heathen land. He founded a monastery on the island, little more than a simple wooden chapel surrounded by a few crude huts, from which he and his followers took their ministry into the surrounding countryside. When Aiden died at Bamburgh in 651, a young lad tending sheep in the nearby hills saw a vision of his soul passing to heaven and was so moved that he journeyed to Melrose Abbey, seeking admittance as a monk. Called Cuthbert, he too

eventually came to Lindisfarne, first as its prior and later, reluctantly, its bishop. Well known for his preaching, Cuthbert developed healing powers and attracted people wherever he went. But his vocation increasingly drew him to prayer and meditation and, in his later years, he withdrew, first to the offshore island here, and then to Inner Farne, where he ended his days.

Cuthbert's body was brought back to Lindisfarne for burial and a cult developed around his memory. Eleven years later, when his body was exhumed to enshrine his bones, the remains were discovered completely undecayed 'as if he were just asleep'. It was to commemorate Cuthbert's elevation to sainthood that the famous *Lindisfarne Gospels* were written, by a monk called Eadfrith, who later also became bishop. The miracles of St Cuthbert drew increasing numbers of pilgrims and the monastery grew both in wealth and influence.

> **WHILE YOU'RE THERE** ⓘ
> As well as the castle and priory, visit the **Lindisfarne Heritage Centre** in Marygate. Displays describe the island's wildlife and man's history since the Stone Age. The highlight, though, is a vivid exhibition of the *Lindisfarne Gospels*.

However, it also attracted unwelcome visitors, the Vikings, and in 875 the monks were forced to abandon the island, taking with them the relics, gospels and even wood from Aiden's original chapel, in search of a new home, which they eventually found at Durham.

WHAT TO LOOK FOR ⓘ

Offshore rocks are often the haunt of basking **grey seals**, the larger of the two species that inhabit Britain's coasts. You'll also see countless birds, in particular the **eider**, or 'Cuddy's' duck, named after St Cuthbert, who offered them protection on Farne. Take a bird guidebook along.

In the 11th century, monks from Durham, by then a Benedictine community, returned to Lindisfarne and refounded the priory, building a church on the site of the chapel where Cuthbert had been buried. About the same time, the parish church was erected and the place became known as Holy Island. At first the monastery prospered, but increasing border hostility at the end of the 13th century ruined the lands upon which it depended. By the Dissolution in 1537, perhaps only a prior and a couple of monks remained here.

The island was first fortified in the 1540s to serve as a landing for raids upon Scotland. It never saw significant action, but remained garrisoned until 1819. In 1901, the publisher Edward Hudson bought the castle and employed Edwin Lutyens in the task of transforming it into a worthy residence. Out of an uninspiring and utilitarian bastion, the architect wrought this intriguing medieval pocket mansion, a fascinating example of the inventiveness and harmony that Lutyens brought to his work.

Head from the car park towards the shore but, just before, at a waymark, turn right through a gate and follow a path on to the reserve. Keep ahead where it later splits, making for the higher dunes in front. Continue past a ruined **lime kiln** and over level ground beyond, to pass through more sandhills before reaching the beach. Head right along the coast, soon crossing an extensive wave-cut platform – go carefully, the rocks may be slippery. Rounding **Snipe Point** into **Coves Haven**, carry on at the head of its sandy beach towards cliffs at the far side. Slippery boulders here need caution, but the way is not difficult. At high tide follow a path above.

Around **Castlehead Rocks**, the going improves along a sandy beach towards the navigation marker on **Emmanuel Head**. There, leave the foreshore and continue at the edge of the dunes towards the castle. Behind it are Bamburgh and the Farne Islands. A raised tram bed, used to feed lime kilns on the left, leads to the castle entrance.

Pass the **castle**, follow a lane towards the village, then bear off left around the harbour. At the jetty, go right to climb on to **The Heugh** behind, turning right along its top past a lookout, Lutyen's stone cross and the ruined **Lantern Chapel**. Beyond, at the bottom, a track on the right climbs back beside **St Mary's Church**. Go into the graveyard and walk around the church to the priory entrance.

Leave the churchyard by its northern gate into the village and walk ahead through **Market Square** to continue along **Crossgate**. Cross over **Marygate** and carry on along **Berwick Road** back to the car park.

Walk 6

Bamburgh's Coast and Castle

Enjoy a fine beach, rolling countryside and superb views to Bamburgh Castle and the Farne Islands.

•DISTANCE•	8½ miles (13.7km)
•MINIMUM TIME•	3hrs 15min
•ASCENT / GRADIENT•	450ft (137m) ▲ ▲ ▲
•LEVEL OF DIFFICULTY•	🚶 🚶 🚶
•PATHS•	Field paths, dunes and beach, 10 stiles
•LANDSCAPE•	Coastal pasture and dunes
•SUGGESTED MAP•	aqua3 OS Explorer 340 Holy Island & Bamburgh
•START / FINISH•	Grid reference: NU 183348
•DOG FRIENDLINESS•	Can be off leads on dunes and beach
•PARKING•	Pay-and-display parking by Bamburgh Castle
•PUBLIC TOILETS•	Bamburgh
•CONTRIBUTOR•	Dennis Kelsall

BACKGROUND TO THE WALK

For as long as people have sailed this coast, the Farne Islands have been a hazard, claiming countless lives on their treacherous rocks. The most easterly outcrop of Northumberland's whinstone intrusion, they form two main groups and comprise around 30 tilted, low-lying islands, some barely breaking the waves. Their harsh environment and isolated position attracted the early Christian saints, who sought seclusion for a life of prayer and meditation. And on Inner Farne, the largest of the group, is a restored 14th-century chapel dedicated to St Cuthbert, who spent the last years of his life there.

The Early Lighthouses

The first attempt to mark the Farne Islands for shipping was around 1673, when a signal fire was lit on a 16th-century tower, built by the Bishop of Durham, on Inner Farne. Later, other beacon towers were built, first on Staple Island and then, in 1783, on Brownsman. The first modern lighthouse was erected on Inner Farne in 1809 and was quickly followed by another on Brownsman. However, the latter actually proved a danger and was replaced in 1826 with one on Longstone. Sadly, even these efficient lights were unable to prevent every disaster, and ships continued to founder on the dangerous reefs. The event that caught the imagination of the country, though, was the wreck of the SS *Forfarshire* in 1838 because of the unstilted heroism of the Longstone keeper and his daughter in rescuing the survivors. The Darlings had been keepers of the Farne lights since 1795, when Robert was appointed to the Brownsman beacon. He later took over the new lighthouse and was followed by his son William in 1815, who then moved to the new light on Longstone when it opened.

An Heroic Rescue

A storm was raging before dawn on 7 September 1838 when the *Forfarshire* struck Big Harcar, just south west of Longstone. William's daughter, Grace, was keeping watch with her father and spotted the wreck, although at first neither could see any survivors. With first light, they sighted men clinging to the wave-washed rock and launched their tiny coble to attempt a rescue. They found nine survivors, including a woman, but were only able to bring five back on the first trip. William returned with two of them for those remaining, whilst his daughter helped the others recover from their exposure. Grace became a national heroine, but managed to remain unaffected by the publicity and stayed with her parents at Bamburgh. Sadly, she died of tuberculosis only four years later at the age of 26. A small museum in the village tells the story and, in the churchyard opposite, there is a replica of the memorial effigy that was placed near her grave, the original having been removed inside the church for protection.

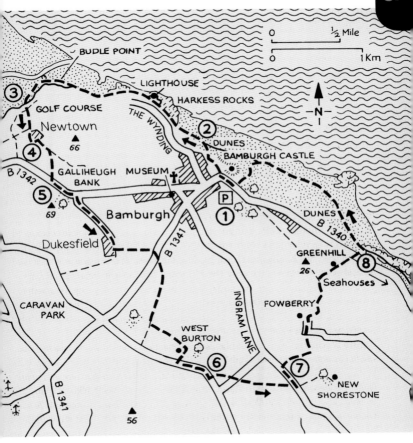

Walk 6 Directions

① Walk towards **Bamburgh** village, where you'll find the museum and church. Our route, however, continues along the beach, reached either across the green below the castle or by following **The Wynding**, just beyond, and then crossing the dunes behind.

② To the left, the sand soon gives way to **Harkess Rocks**. Carefully pick your way round to the **lighthouse** at Blackrocks Point,

Walk 6

which is more easily negotiated to the landward side. Continue below the dunes, shortly regaining a sandy beach to pass around **Budle Point**.

③ Shortly before a derelict pier, climb on to the dunes towards a World War Two gun emplacement, behind which a waymarked path rises on to a golf course. Continue past markers to a gate, leaving along a track above a caravan park. At a bend, go through a gate on the left (marked 'Private') and carry on at the edge of the field to reach the cottages at **Newtown**.

④ Beyond, follow a wall on the left to regain the golf course over a stile at the top field-corner. Bear right to pass left of a look-out and continue on a grass track to the main road.

⑤ Walk down **Galliheugh Bank** to a bend and turn off to **Dukesfield**. Approaching the lane's end, go left

over a stile, walk past a house to the field's far corner and continue by a hedge to a road. Cross to follow a green lane opposite and eventually, just after a cottage, reach a stile on the left. Make for **West Burton farm**, turn right through the farmyard to a lane and then go left.

⑥ Beyond a bend and over a stile on the left, signed 'New Shorestone', bear half-right across a field. Emerging on to a quiet lane, go over another stile opposite and continue in the same direction to **Ingram Lane**.

⑦ Some 300yds to the left (274m), a gated track on the right leads away and then around to the left towards **Fowberry**. Meeting a narrow lane, go left to the farm, then turn right immediately before the entrance on to a green track. In the next field, follow the left perimeter around the corner to a metal gate. Through that, remain beside the right-hand wall to a double gate, there turning right across a final field to **Greenhill**. Keep ahead to the main road.

⑧ Continue across to the beach and head north to Bamburgh. Approaching the castle, turn inland, over the dunes, where a cattle fence can be crossed by one of several gates or stiles. Work your way through to regain the road by the car park.

Kirknewton and Ancient Yeavering Bell

Views of the Cheviot Hills and the sea are the reward for climbing to this hilltop fort.

•DISTANCE•	5 miles (8km)
•MINIMUM TIME•	2hrs 15min
•ASCENT / GRADIENT•	1,115ft (340m) ▲▲▲
•LEVEL OF DIFFICULTY•	🚶 🚶 🚶
•PATHS•	Tracks, field paths and moorland, steep ascent and descent
•LANDSCAPE•	Farmland and hillside, wide views from Yeavering Bell
•SUGGESTED MAP•	aqua3 OS Explorer OL16 The Cheviot Hills
•START / FINISH•	Grid reference: NT 914302
•DOG FRIENDLINESS•	Dogs on leads
•PARKING•	In Kirknewton village, in wide area of road beyond school and church, off B6351
•PUBLIC TOILETS•	None on route
•CONTRIBUTOR•	David Winpenny

BACKGROUND TO THE WALK

The village of Kirknewton huddles at the foot of the Cheviot Hills, close to the beautiful valley of the College Burn. Often used as a stopping-off point for walkers, the village itself deserves exploration. It has some old farmhouses and a deceptive church, which appears Victorian but contains a chancel with a stone roof that curves to the floor like the hull of an upturned ship. By the arch leading to the chancel is Kirknewton's other treasure – a 12th-century carving of the Wise Men visiting the infant Jesus and his mother. It is roughly carved and has an almost cartoon-like quality, but is a fascinating and moving glimpse into a world nearly 1,000 years ago.

A Victorian Reformer

A memorial in Kirknewton church remembers Josephine Butler, the 19th-century social reformer, who is buried in the churchyard. She was born near by in 1828 and married George Butler, a lecturer at Durham University. They moved to Oxford after they married but, following the death of their five-year-old daughter, they set up home in Liverpool, where Josephine began her life's work of helping rescue women from prostitution and the 'white slave' trade. Her campaign included direct physical action against what she considered unfair laws, which were eventually repealed. She based her life on prayer and modelled herself on St Catherine of Sienna. She retired to Northumberland in 1890, after George's death, and died in 1906.

College Valley

The first part of the walk skirts West Hill, which is topped by a small hill fort with a stone wall and the remains of a Romano-British settlement. You will then pass the head of the beautiful College Valley – it is possible to drive down beyond Hethpool only with a special free permit from Sale and Partners at 18–20 Glendale Road in Wooler. Only 12 a day are issued, and none in the lambing season from mid-April to the end of May. It is open to walkers at any time.

The climax of the walk is the hill fort at Yeavering Bell. Northumberland's most spectacular Iron-Age structure, the fort has a massive rubble wall, once 10ft (3m) thick at the base, surrounding the two peaks of the hill. The 13½ acres (5.5ha) within held more than 130 timber buildings, the largest of them 42ft (12.8m) across. Below the hill, just east of Kirknewton, once stood Ad Gefrin, the 7th-century palace of King Edwin. Mentioned in Bede's *Ecclesiastical History of the English People*, the site was lost for centuries until identified by crop marks in 1949, and then excavated. St Paulinus baptised converts in the River Glen near by in AD 627, and probably preached in Ad Gefrin's most unusual feature, an open-air wooden theatre that held more than 300 people.

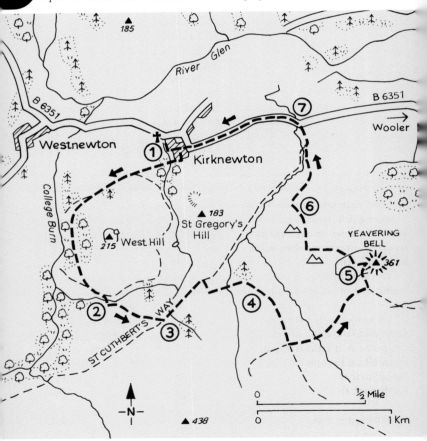

Walk 7 Directions

① From the parking place, walk ahead towards the village centre, then turn left. Just before a gate,

bend right along the lane, following the 'Hillforts Trail' sign. The metalled lane bends right again and becomes a grassy track. Go through a metal gate and straight on at the next waymarker. Go through two

Walk 7

more metal gates and a gateway. At the next marker post bear right, signed 'Permissive Path' and go over a stream and a ladder stile.

② Turn left after the stile, then go over another stile. Bear half right across the field to a hand gate in a crossing wall, Go through the gate, and bear right to reach a waymarked post beside the track. This is part of **St Cuthbert's Way**.

③ Turn left along the track and follow it through a wooden waymarked gate, past a farmhouse and over a cattle grid. Just before the next cattle grid turn right off the track, following the 'St Cuthbert's Way' sign. Bend left through a gate and continue along the grassy track uphill to a ladder stile in the wall on your left.

④ Go over the stile and turn right to follow the footpath uphill. At a low-level signpost, turn left, signed 'Yeavering Bell'. Follow the waymarks down into the valley, across the stream and then uphill. The path eventually passes through the fort wall. Bend right to reach the summit of **Yeavering Bell**.

⑤ After enjoying the view, go downhill to the valley between the two peaks. Bear right and head downhill, on the opposite side of the hill to that which you came up. Go through the wall and follow the

WHILE YOU'RE THERE

For a taste of genuine Northumberland farming life visit nearby **Wooler**. Set on the first slopes of the Cheviot Hills, it is a pleasant town, and the centre for a wide area. It has long held a cattle market, and the shops mix guides and souvenirs for tourists with agricultural supplies.

waymark just beyond. The path is waymarked all the way down the steep hill, until you reach a stile.

⑥ Go over the stile, and then over a ladder stile on your right on to a track. Follow the track past a marker post and, just after it, bend left towards another track, which leads towards the farm buildings in the valley bottom. Go over a ladder stile by the buildings and turn right along the track. Go through a metal gate and past the cottages to reach the road.

WHERE TO EAT AND DRINK

Head for Wooler, where there is a wide choice of pubs and cafés. The **Black Bull** and the **Red Lion** are recommended, while the **Tankerville Arms** has a good reputation for its food. All welcome dogs; children are welcome at the Black Bull and Tankerville Arms.

⑦ Turn left along the road and follow it back to **Kirknewton**. At the 'Yetholm' sign at the entrance to the village go straight ahead, through the gate, then turn right back to the car.

WHAT TO LOOK FOR

Part of the walk follows the long distance footpath called **St Cuthbert's Way**. The 62½-mile (100km) route goes eastwards from Melrose in the Scottish Borders, where St Cuthbert first began his monastic life, into England, finishing at Holy Island off the Northumberland coast (► Walk 5). Cuthbert is one of the most famous of the early English saints, and much revered in the north of England. His shrine in Durham Cathedral, where his bones were taken more than a century after they were rescued by the Holy Island monks during Danish raids in 875, was long a place of pilgrimage. Cuthbert's coffin and cross are in the cathedral's treasury.

Walk 8

The Wild Cattle of Chillingham

A walk that encircles a haunted castle and the home of the only wild cattle left in Britain.

•DISTANCE•	6 miles (9.7km)
•MINIMUM TIME•	3hrs
•ASCENT / GRADIENT•	754ft (230m) ▲▲▲
•LEVEL OF DIFFICULTY•	🚶🚶 🚶🚶 🚶
•PATHS•	Hill track, surfaced road
•LANDSCAPE•	Hill, arable and woodland
•SUGGESTED MAP•	aqua3 OS Explorer 340 Holy Island & Bamburgh
•START / FINISH•	Grid reference: NU 071248
•DOG FRIENDLINESS•	Dogs not allowed in Chillingham Wood, even on lead
•PARKING•	Forest car park at Hepburn Wood
•PUBLIC TOILETS•	None on route
•CONTRIBUTOR•	Anthony Toole

BACKGROUND TO THE WALK

The origins of the Chillingham wild cattle are not known. Their skull structure suggests similarities with the aurochs, so they may be descended from those ancient wild oxen that once roamed Britain. Recent DNA tests performed on dead animals show that they are unrelated to any other European cattle. Having remained uncontaminated by outside stock, they are probably the only genetically pure cattle in the world. They are always white, no coloured animals have ever been born, and they are definitely wild.

Captured Cattle

The Chillingham herd has roamed its 365-acre (148ha) park for almost 700 years, since Sir Thomas Percy was granted a royal licence to fortify Chillingham Castle and enclose the grounds. The captured cattle may have provided a food supply. Over the years they have never been domesticated. The strongest bull leads the herd, he remains 'King', and sires all the calves born during his 'rule' until such time as another bull successfully challenges him. Even a birth is accompanied by a ritual, which must be observed before the new calf is accepted into the herd.

Care of the Herd

The number of cattle in the herd normally varies from 40 to 60, but during the severe winter of 1947, their numbers fell to 13. Their wild nature meant that normal agricultural methods could not be employed to help them. The Chillingham cattle never seek shelter other than in the surrounding trees and will eat only grass and hay and, even when starving, will not accept oats or prepared cattle food. Fortunately the cattle are rarely ill, but when disease does strike, they cannot be approached by a vet. The tragic outbreak of foot and mouth disease in 1967 and again in 2001 threatened the survival of the herd, on the earlier occasion encroaching within 2 miles (3.2km) of Chillingham.

Walk 8

The Chillingham Wild Cattle Association was formed in 1939 to look after the welfare of the herd. The 8th Earl of Tankerville bequeathed ownership of the herd to the association on his death in 1971. When the 9th earl died in 1980, the Chillingham Estate was put up for sale. As a result of the intervention of the Duke of Northumberland, Chillingham Park was sold separately from the castle to the Sir James Knott Charitable Trust, which granted the association grazing rights for 999 years.

Visitors can see the cattle in their natural surroundings, which look much as they did in medieval times. The cattle's behaviour, however, is unpredictable, so for safety reasons, you can only enter the park when accompanied by the warden. Binoculars are recommended for a close view. The park is open daily except Tuesday and the entrance fee is relatively modest.

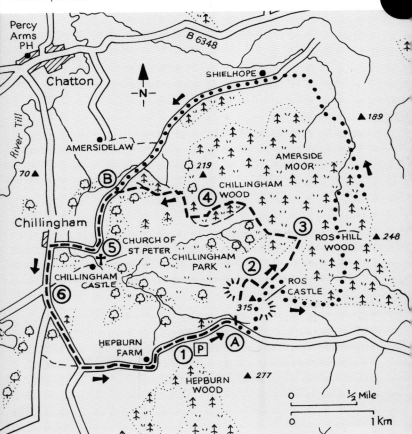

Walk 8 Directions

① On leaving the car park, turn right on to the road and go uphill for ½ mile (800m) and round a bend to a National Trust notice

indicating Ros Castle (Point Ⓐ on Walk 9). Follow the track to a gate in the wall to your left and go through the gate into **Chillingham Wood**. Turn right, then left and follow marker posts on to a broader track after 100yds (90m). This leads

Walk 8

you uphill, then across a level stretch to a fence. On your left is a view over Chillingham Park, where you might, on occasion, be able to see the wild cattle.

② Turn right at the fence and go uphill as indicated by the signpost to Chillingham. When you reach the wall, turn left and follow the track between the wall and the fence to a picnic table. Continue to the next forest, and walk between the wall and the forest for about 250yds (229m) to the next signpost to Chillingham.

③ Turn left and descend through the forest, following the marker posts about 50yds (46m) apart. When this small track reaches a junction with a track signed 'Forest Way', turn right and continue to a signpost pointing to Amerside Moor and Chillingham. Take the Chillingham direction, through two tall kissing gates to a picnic area with two tables.

④ Continue along the track to a forest road and turn right on to this, which becomes metalled lower down. When you reach a sign pointing left over a small bridge to the Forest Walk, ignore this and instead go through the gate and along the road out of the forest. (Point Ⓑ, Walk 9). The road you are now on leads to the entrance to **Chillingham Park**.

⑤ Follow the road past the **Church of St Peter**, on your left, then past a gate leading to **Chillingham Castle**. Cross the **Hollow Burn** either by ford or footbridge and continue to a T-junction with the main road. Turn left and follow the road, passing the main castle gate after 550yds (500m).

⑥ At the next fork in the road, take the left fork and go uphill to the crossroads. This road is not very busy with traffic and has good grass verges for walking on. Turn left on to the road to **Hepburn Farm**. Follow this, past the farm buildings, and continue to **Hepburn Wood** car park.

Ros Castle and Chillingham

Extend the walk for a more energetic ramble past a superb viewpoint.
See map and information panel for Walk 8

•DISTANCE•	9 miles (14.5km)
•MINIMUM TIME•	4hrs 30min
•ASCENT / GRADIENT•	820ft (250m) ▲▲▲
•LEVEL OF DIFFICULTY•	🚶🚶 🚶🚶 🚶🚶

Walk 9 Directions (Walk 8 option)

From Point Ⓐ on Walk 8, by the NT sign for Ros Castle, continue along the road for a further 220yds (200m). Follow the obvious track up the hill on your left. Where the track forks, take the left option and go up to the **trig point**.

The remains of **Ros Castle**, a 3,000-year old hill fort, lie around the summit. From the viewing platform you can see seven historic castles: Lindisfarne, Bamburgh, Dunstanburgh, Warkworth, Alnwick, Ford and Chillingham.

Follow the wall down the far side of the hill, then up again to reach a fence. Follow the fence downhill to your right. When the bracken is high, the track may be difficult to find, but progress becomes easier from the bottom of the hill.

At the entrance to **Ros Hill Wood**, cross the stile and go into the forest. The track leads to a clearing after 200yds (183m). Cross this and continue in the same direction. Go past the first junction, where a firebreak leads to the right. At the second firebreak, turn right and follow the track for ¼ mile (400m) to a fence at the edge of the forest. The track is good, but the tree branches extend over it in places. Open heather moorland lies beyond the fence, with a communications tower about ¾ mile (1.2km) away.

Turn left and follow the track by the fence to a sharp corner at the end of the forest. On the right is a small tarn. Climb over the wooden corner of the fence into a field and follow the fence for 330yds (300m) to a junction with a footpath by a gate.

Cross the field to your left. The footpath is indefinite, so aim for the left end of the gorse that fringes the river valley to your right. There, you will cross a concrete pipe on to a track between two fences. Continue to a metal gate, go through this and turn left and through another gate. Follow the field edge, through a third gate and past wooden sheep enclosures. The track passes **Shielhope**, right, and continues to a forest, curving round to the left, past a junction with a concrete road leading to **Amersidelaw farm**.

Continue in the same direction, through metal gates and over a wooden gate into the next forest. About 500yds (450m) through this, you will reach Point Ⓑ on Walk 8.

Walk 10

Alnwick's Hulne Park

The parkland estate of the Dukes of Northumberland, with an 18th-century prospect tower and two former monasteries.

•DISTANCE•	8 miles (12.9km)
•MINIMUM TIME•	2hrs 45min
•ASCENT / GRADIENT•	886ft (270m) ▲▲▲
•LEVEL OF DIFFICULTY•	秩 秩 秩
•PATHS•	Well-surfaced tracks, with a few field paths
•LANDSCAPE•	Parkland and woodland
•SUGGESTED MAP•	aqua3 OS Explorer 332 Alnwick & Amble
•START / FINISH•	Grid reference: NU 185135
•DOG FRIENDLINESS•	Dogs on leads
•PARKING•	In Bailiffgate in Alnwick, near castle
•PUBLIC TOILETS•	In Market Place and by coach park
•NOTE•	Hulne Park open 11AM to sunset most days of year
•CONTRIBUTOR•	David Winpenny

Walk 10 Directions

From **Bailiffgate** walk towards Alnwick Castle, home of the Percy family, Dukes of Northumberland. Often called the 'Windsor of the North', its warlike exterior – seen on-screen in the Harry Potter films – hides rich Renaissance-style interiors. Turn left down **The Peth**, and go over the **Lion Bridge**, with its stiff-tailed Percy lion, the family's crest. In the pastures below the castle an annual Shrove Tuesday football match takes place. Teams representing the rival parishes of

St Michael and St Paul battle it out, with the Lion Bridge and Denwick Bridge, ¾ mile (1.2km) east, as the goalposts. Begin to ascend the hill, and at a sign 'Abbeylands', turn left. Go through two kissing gates, then on a track between houses, which winds to a road.

Turn left down the road. To the right, beside the river, is the 15th-century gatehouse of Alnwick Abbey, the only remnant of a Premonstratensian monastery founded in 1147. Go over the bridge, then through a gate on the right, signed 'Ratten Row'. Follow the lane to another gate then up the field and out on to a lane. Turn right through the archway into **Hulne Park**, which was landscaped in the 18th century by Lancelot 'Capability' Brown.

Follow the drive ahead, crossing a bridge and following the **Farm Drive**. Pass the **Park Farm** entrance (to which you will return) and,

> ### WHILE YOU'RE THERE ⓘ
> Explore the town of **Alnwick**. Don't miss the narrow Hotspur Gate, named after the most famous of the Percys, and the Old Cross Inn, with the display of old bottles in the window, unaltered since a landlord died while arranging them over 150 years ago. In the former railway station is one of Britain's largest secondhand bookshops.

¼ mile (400m) beyond, turn left opposite a small hut up a blue-waymarked track. Follow the track uphill, going straight on where the path divides. **Brizlee Tower** is on your right near the top of the hill. The 78ft (23.7m) tall tower is carefully placed to take in views to the Cheviot Hills and towards the coast. It was designed by Robert Adam for the 1st Duke.

WHERE TO EAT AND DRINK

There is a variety of places in Alnwick. Those who wish to imagine themselves as Kate Winslet or Leonardo Di Caprio could head for the **White Swan Hotel** on Bondgate Within, not far from the Hotspur Gate. A visit to its Olympic Room is like being aboard the *Titanic*, for the *Olympic* was *Titanic*'s sister ship, and the room's fittings came from her when she was broken up in 1935.

Return the same way – there are views towards Alnwick Castle – and turn right by the hut, back to the **Park Farm** entrance. Turn left towards the farm, then after 50yds (46m) turn left on to the green-waymarked trail into the woods. The track goes through trees to a gate, then though grassland to another gate and an iron bridge, constructed by Cookson of Newcastle in 1812. After the bridge turn right, towards **Hulne Priory**, then turn off the track uphill to its entrance. The earliest Carmelite monastery in England, Hulne is surrounded by a strong wall that hides a pretty garden. You can still see the ruins of the church, chapter house, sacristy and refectory, while the former infirmary is now a private house. In the 18th century a summerhouse was added in the corner of the cloisters, linked by an arch to the thick-walled tower, built in 1486.

After visiting the priory, turn right out of its entrance. The track bends to a gate in a wall. Turn right at the next green waymark, and then right again, going downhill to meet a crossing track. Turn left and follow the track beside the river. Go through an orange-waymarked gate, cross a bridge with a gate at the end, and go ahead, still following the orange waymarks. Turn left over the next bridge, again with a gate, and pass a stone inscribed 'Alnwick Abbey Drive'. At the next orange waymark, turn right through a gate and over a waymarked footbridge, known as the **Duchess's Bridge**. When you reach a T-junction of paths, turn left along a wider track. Follow it through woodland to an open triangular area. Go straight ahead, and over a stone bridge, then bear left, uphill. Turn left at the top and follow the metalled road straight ahead, through the arch and past the church back into **Bailiffgate**.

WHAT TO LOOK FOR

Winter walkers in Hulne Park may be rewarded by the sight of **bramblings**. They fly in from their homelands in the birch and beech forests of Scandinavia and Russia, often when food is scarce there. About 6in (15cm) long, they resemble chaffinches, but have a white rump, particularly visible when they are flying. Look out for them near beech trees, as this is where they feed. You may also spot the **snow bunting**, another winter visitor this time from Greenland and Scandinavia. Although they favour sand or shingle coastlines, they have been seen in Alnwick and are easy to spot because they are mostly white and around 6½in (16.5cm) long. They feed in flocks and, in flight, they have been compared to drifting snowflakes.

Burned Hamlets of the Breamish

A walk that captures the essence of Northumberland's most beautiful valley.

•DISTANCE•	5 miles (8km)
•MINIMUM TIME•	2hrs 30min (add another hour for detours)
•ASCENT / GRADIENT•	590ft (180m) ▲▲▲
•LEVEL OF DIFFICULTY•	👫 👫 👫
•PATHS•	Part metalled road, part hill tracks, 1 stile
•LANDSCAPE•	Hills, river valleys and woodland
•SUGGESTED MAP•	aqua3 OS Explorer OL16 The Cheviot Hills
•START / FINISH•	Grid reference: NT 976162
•DOG FRIENDLINESS•	Keep on lead through farmland and near sheep
•PARKING•	Roadside parking at Hartside
•PUBLIC TOILETS•	None on route, nearest at Bulby's wood picnic area, ¾ mile (1.2km) west of Ingram
•CONTRIBUTOR•	Anthony Toole

BACKGROUND TO THE WALK

It is a river with two names. As the Breamish, it trickles from the peat of the Cheviots. After flowing through narrow V-shaped gorges, past the hamlets of Linhope, Hartside and Ingram, it swings north, changing its name to the Till somewhere near Wooler. A few miles further it joins the Tweed and finally meets the sea at Berwick.

Cushat Law and Bloodybush Edge
Both of the river's names are Celtic in origin, while those of the hamlets and the surrounding hills bear the more staccato syllables of an Anglo-Saxon overlay that reflects the history of the valley itself. Names like Cushat Law (Woodpigeon Hill) and Bloodybush Edge, and the growth of wood sorrel on springtime slopes tell of the forests and birch scrub that covered the now grassy hilltops a thousand years ago.

Breamish Valley
It was the coming of agriculture, and in particular the grazing of sheep, that cleared the hills of their trees. The farms of the now sparsely populated Breamish Valley, once supported large, thriving communities. First came the Celts, who built settlements on the rounded summits with commanding views over the valley. Ewe Hill, Brough Law and Hartside Hill, to the west of Ingram village all held extensive constructions, the ruins of which can easily be seen, while to the south of Linhope are the remains of several smaller dwellings on Meggrim's Knowe.

Grieve's Ash
On the hill that overlooks Linhope from the north, are the remains of the hut circles and fortifications of Grieve's Ash. Covering an area of 20 acres (8.1ha), this was the largest Romano-British settlement in Northumbria. A translation of its name appears to refer to a

burned hamlet whose Celtic inhabitants were subject to the Saxon Greve, or District Governor. Perhaps this governor burned the village as a reprisal for some misdemeanour.

Ingram's name is derived from the Anglo-Saxon 'angr', which refers to the grasslands that provided excellent grazing for sheep. As the population grew, and land on the valley floor became scarce, cultivation terraces, or lynchets were constructed on the hillsides. These varied in length from 55yds (50m) to 220yds (200m) and were up to 5yds (5m) wide. Surface boulders were used to build low retaining walls and the land behind these was levelled and ploughed.

In addition to the usual moorland species like lapwing, curlew, red grouse and pheasant, visitors to the Breamish Valley are also likely to see oystercatchers, barn owls and merlins. A few years ago, a red kite took up temporary residence near Linhope.

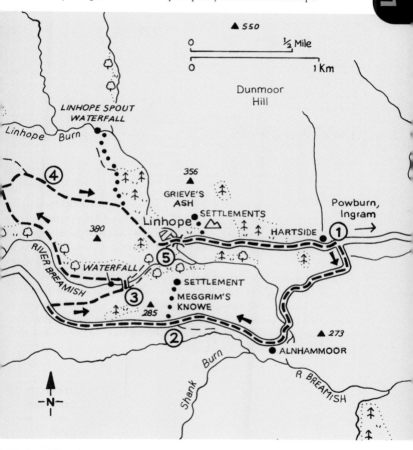

Walk 11 **Directions**

① From **Hartside**, take the metalled road signposted to Alnhammoor, over a cattle grid, then turn sharp right and go downhill. At the bottom of the hill, the road turns left and leads you to a wooden bridge. Cross the bridge and continue steadily uphill, past the farm and across three more cattle grids. The impressive river valley is to your left.

② Near the top of the first rise, another track joins the main roadway from the left. You are now on the side of **Meggrim's Knowe**. (A relatively simple, though trackless, detour over the hill to your right and down to a shoulder on the other side will bring you, in about ¼ mile (400m) to the remains of the Celtic settlement.) Continue on the metalled road, passing a small wood on your right, and carry on over the next rise to reach a dip in the road. At the bottom of this dip, turn right on to a prominent grassy track that leads downhill to the valley floor and a footbridge over the **River Breamish**.

WHERE TO EAT AND DRINK ⓘ

Very light refreshments only can be bought at the **Ingram National Park Centre**. More substantial meals can be eaten at the **Poacher's Rest Coffee House and Restaurant** at the Hedgeley Service Station on the A697 just north of Powburn. In Powburn village itself, the **Plough** serves bar meals.

---

③ Cross the footbridge and the low stile, then turn left along the track, passing a small waterfall after about 220yds (201m). Continue across an open stretch of land, lined along the riverbank with copper beeches, go through the gate and uphill past new oak and rowan woodland. A second gate gives access to open hillside. A few hundred paces after this, the track becomes grassy and can be a little swampy in places. Continue for a further ¼ mile (400m) to join a track leading from the left. Turn right along this to another track and again go right to a fence.

④ Go through the gate and down to the side of the forest, passing through another gate on the way. **Linhope Spout** can be reached by following the lower track along the forest edge, through a kissing gate and downhill for ¼ mile (400m). This is a short but very rewarding detour. Back on the main route, follow the rubble track to the right to reach **Linhope** village after ¼ mile (400m).

WHILE YOU'RE THERE ⓘ

Adjacent to the National Park Centre in Ingram is the **Church of St Michael** – parts of the walls of the church date back to Norman times. About a mile (1.6km) to the north west of Linhope, a tributary of the Breamish tumbles over a 50ft (15m) crag of volcanic rock into a deep pool, to form **Linhope Spout**, possibly the most picturesque waterfall in the whole of Northumberland.

---

⑤ The metalled road leads across a bridge and uphill for 220yds (200m) to where a broad track on the left leads into a field at the side of the forest. To visit **Grieve's Ash**, go on to this track, then follow the edge of the forest steeply uphill for 110yds (100m). The extensive remains of the settlement occupy the whole area behind the forest. The main road leads you back to **Hartside** in about ½ mile (800m).

WHAT TO LOOK FOR ⓘ

Cultivation terraces, or **lynchets** are plainly visible just north of where the road forks, about ¾ mile (1.2km) east of Ingram. More can be seen on the hillsides to the south west of Ingram and can be reached, in ½ mile (800m), by means of a track from the western end of the village.

Through the Gorge of the River Coquet

A fairly demanding but spectacular walk through Northumberland's geological history.

•DISTANCE•	4½ miles (7.2km)
•MINIMUM TIME•	3hrs
•ASCENT / GRADIENT•	590ft (180m) ▲▲▲
•LEVEL OF DIFFICULTY•	🚶🚶 🚶🚶 🚶🚶
•PATHS•	Mostly hill footpaths, 8 stiles
•LANDSCAPE•	Hills and river gorge
•SUGGESTED MAP•	aqua3 OS Explorer OL16 The Cheviot Hills
•START / FINISH•	Grid reference: NT 919063
•DOG FRIENDLINESS•	Keep on lead on road and near sheep on hills
•PARKING•	Car park at Alwinton
•PUBLIC TOILETS•	At car park
•NOTE•	Close to MOD artillery range over Barrow Scar. When red flags flying, walk may be inadvisable. Contact Range Control Officer on 01830 520569 or 0191 239 4261
•CONTRIBUTOR•	Anthony Toole

BACKGROUND TO THE WALK

The oldest rocks in Northumberland, older even than the Alps, are those of the Cheviot Hills. They were formed by volcanic activity, which began about 380 million years ago, and once rose to heights in excess of 15,000ft (4,572m). Relentless weathering has worn down the mountains and rounded their summits, so that Cheviot itself, the highest peak, is now only 2,677ft (816m) high. The heat and pressure of further eruptions sometimes cooked and hardened the earlier rocks, so that they became more resistant to erosion and now stand as craggy tors above the Breamish and Harthope valleys.

Sedimentary Rocks

Shallow seas then washed the feet of the mountains and aided their erosion. Deposits of mud and sand were laid down and compacted into shales and sandstones. The living creatures of these seas extracted calcium salts from the water to form their shells and bones, which then added to the sediments as chalk and limestone. The successive layers of sedimentary rock are known as the cementstones and are around 340 million years old.

Fell Sandstones

After the the formation of the cementstones, the whole area became the delta of a vast river that flowed out of a North Atlantic landmass. The coarse-grained sands from this formed a layer 500–1,000ft (152–305m) thick. This became the fell sandstones that cover much of central Northumberland. Emperor Hadrian used these hard rocks to build his wall. Later, men like John Dobson, used them to construct many of Newcastle's buildings, of which the Central Railway Station is a good example.

Formation of the Valleys

The most recent period of geological activity, beginning about one million years ago, has been characterised by the ice ages, during which ice sheets covered Northumberland's hills, to a height of 2,000ft (610m). Glaciers, several hundred feet thick carved broad U-shaped valleys in the hills. After their retreat came the rivers, which continue their erosion to the present day, seaming the hillsides with narrow, V-shaped valleys that have slowly exposed the rocks of the different geological eras.

The Coquet Gorge

Nowhere is Northumberland's geological history better laid out to view than around the gorge of the River Coquet, west of the village of Alwinton. To the north are the volcanic Cheviot Hills, while to the south are the fell sandstones. And in the gorge itself, at Barrow Scar, the layers of the cementstones lie fully exposed.

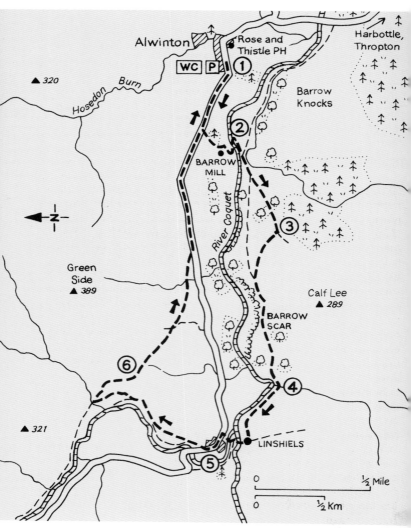

Walk 12 Directions

① Turn right, out of the car park and follow the road for 700yds (640m) to a gate on the left leading to **Barrow Mill**. Go through the gate and down to the farm, passing the remains of a corn-drying kiln that dates from 1812. Go through another gate into a field, cross this and go through a gate to the river bank. Ford the river. After a period of rain, this will involve getting your feet wet.

WHILE YOU'RE THERE

At **Harbottle** are the remains of a castle built in the reign of Henry II as defence against the Scots. Lady's Well, at Holystone, was built by the Romans around a spring that was used for early Christian baptisms. Bishop Paulinus is said to have baptised 2,000 people here on Easter Sunday, AD 627.

② Enter the field and follow the fence to the right to a gate. Go through this or over the stile about 20yds (18m) away to the left and continue to the derelict farm buildings. Follow the track up the hillside to the right-hand corner of the conifer forest.

③ About 50yds (46m) before reaching a signpost marking the edge of a military firing range, follow a less well-defined track across the heather-covered hillside to the right, rising slightly, until you come to a wire fence. Follow this over the top of **Barrow Scar**, keeping the fence on your right. When you meet a second fence, follow this to a stile. Cross the stile and go down to an obvious loop in the river. In late summer, the bracken here may be deep and the track obscured.

④ At the river bend, cross a stile, then another after a further 100yds (91m). Cross over the field and a stile into the farmyard at **Linshiels**. Go through the farmyard, across two bridges and join the road. Turn left and follow the road until just past the farm buildings, to a signpost pointing to Shillmoor.

WHERE TO EAT AND DRINK

The **Rose and Thistle**, Alwinton, is a good pub, but does not serve meals. Sandwiches and side salad are served at the **Star**, Harbottle, at lunch times only. Try the bar meals at the **Three Wheat Heads** or at the **Cross Keys**, Thropton, 8 miles (12.9km) from Alwinton.

⑤ Go up the hillside, over a stile and follow the track overlooking the gorge and its waterfalls. This is the most spectacular part of the walk. For a short distance, the slopes below are quite precipitous and care is needed, though the track is good. When the track splits, keep to the higher branch and go round the hillside to join a more prominent track leading up from the left. Turn right and follow this track uphill.

⑥ At the top of the slope continue across level ground, then descend to a stile. Cross this and follow the track, over another stile and down to the road. Follow the road for 1 mile (1.6km) back to **Alwinton**.

WHAT TO LOOK FOR

The first half of the walk is over **fell sandstone**, the second over **volcanic rock**. As well as rock textures, note the different vegetation: grassy and bracken-covered on the volcanic slopes, heathery on the more acidic fell sandstones. The layered structure of the cementstones at Barrow Scar is well observed from the second part of the walk.

Craster and a Ruined Castle

From a village famous for its kippers to a castle that inspired Turner.

·DISTANCE·	5 miles (8km)
·MINIMUM TIME·	1hr 45min
·ASCENT / GRADIENT·	275ft (84m)
·LEVEL OF DIFFICULTY·	
·PATHS·	Generally good tracks, some field paths tussocky, 1 stile
·LANDSCAPE·	Coastal pasture and dunes
·SUGGESTED MAP·	aqua3 OS Explorer 332 Alnwick & Amble
·START / FINISH·	Grid reference: NU 256198
·DOG FRIENDLINESS·	On lead through village and by coast; sheep grazing
·PARKING·	Pay-and-display behind Craster tourist information centre
·PUBLIC TOILETS·	Beside information centre
·CONTRIBUTOR·	Dennis Kelsall

BACKGROUND TO THE WALK

Standing in dramatic isolation on a craggy outcrop of whinstone cliff, and overlooking the vast emptiness of the North Sea, is one of England's most spectacular medieval ruins, Dunstanburgh Castle. Its lonely silhouette has inspired several artists, such as the great landscape painter J M W Turner, and the castle's atmospheric shell featured as a set in the film version of *Hamlet* (1991) starring Mel Gibson and Glenn Close.

A Fine Castle

Building began around 1313 by Thomas, Earl of Lancaster, the richest and most powerful baron of his day and a fierce opponent of his cousin, Edward II. Edward, though, upset more than Lancaster at his court, by his devotion to Piers Gaveston, son of a Gascon nobleman. After Edward created Gaveston Earl of Cornwall, Lancaster mustered an opposition that contrived the execution of the King's favourite for treason. However, Lancaster's popularity amongst the other barons waned and he met his own sticky end after leaving the security of his Dunstanburgh stronghold to venture south in an ill-conceived alliance with the Scots. Meeting the King's forces at Boroughbridge, his army was routed and Lancaster captured. Rank brought him no protection from the regal wrath and, six days later, the King avenged the death of his friend Gaveston by the execution of Lancaster, also on charges of treason.

The outer curtain walls of the castle cover more than 9 acres (3.6ha), exploiting the natural defences of a high, sheer sea cliff to the north and a craggy coast to the east. The steep western flank of the outcrop presented its own difficulties for would-be assailants. Part of the original construction, the outer wall is 10ft (3m) thick in places and was entered by a massive three-storey gatehouse protected by two towers rising high above. A later Earl of Lancaster, John of Gaunt, converted this gatehouse into the keep and built an alternative entrance further along the outer wall, although of this nothing but the foundations remain.

Other additions included the Lilburn Tower on the western wall, serving as a look-out and defence against land attack from the north, whilst the south and east were protected by the Constable's and Egyncleugh towers. However, although the mighty fortress must have appeared an impregnable defence against the military strategy and war engines of its day, it was not designed to withstand the cannon that followed. The castle was besieged during the 1460s in the Wars of the Roses as the Yorkists moved to gain control in Northumberland and suffered a pounding at the hands of Richard Neville, Earl of Warwick. It was never re-fortified and quietly crumbled to become the splendid ruin seen today.

Walk 13 Directions

① From the car park, turn right towards the village. Immediately before the harbour, go left into **Dunstanburgh Road**, signed 'Castle', and carry on through a gate

at the end above a rocky shore towards **Dunstanburgh Castle**.

② After two more gates, if you want to visit the castle, keep to the main track, which winds around to its entrance. Otherwise, bear left on a less-distinct path through a shallow gorge on the landward side. Continuing below the castle, the ruins of the **Lilburn Tower**, perched dramatically on top of a rocky spur outcrop, are an impressive feature.

③ Beyond, as you pass above a bouldery beach, glance back to the cliffs protecting Dunstanburgh Castle's northern aspect, which, in the early summer, echo to the screams of innumerable seabirds, squabbling for nesting sites on the narrow ledges.

> **WHAT TO LOOK FOR** ⓘ
>
> Wandering through Craster, your nose is sure to lure you to **Robinson's Smokehouse**, where kipper-making has been a family business for four generations. Famed throughout the country, they are cured in a traditional manner and, although the herrings are no longer landed at Craster harbour, the kippers are as good as any you will find.

④ Through a kissing gate at the edge of a golf course, bear right to remain above the shore, where dramatic folding of the rocks is plainly evident. Ahead stretches the sandy expanse of **Embleton Bay** and, if the tide permits, you can continue along the beach.

⑤ Shortly, look for a prominent break in the dunes, through which a path leads across the golf course to meet a lane. Follow it up to **Dunstan Steads**, turning left immediately before on to a drive, signed 'Dunstan Square'. Where this bends behind the buildings, bear left across an open area to a gate and continue over the open fields on a farm track.

⑥ After a mile (1.6km), at **Dunstan Square**, pass through two successive gates by a barn and then turn left

> **WHILE YOU'RE THERE** ⓘ
>
> The nearby **Howick Estate** has been held by the Grey family since 1319 and, although the 18th-century hall is not open to the public, its beautiful grounds are. Woodland walks and formal gardens have been thoughtfully designed to capture attention throughout the seasons. From April until June there is a spectacular display of azalea, rhododendron and magnolia. Later, your attention is focussed upon herbaceous borders, which provide colour until the woodland and ornamental trees don their autumnal cloaks.

through a third gate, signed 'Craster'. Walk down the field edge, through another gate at the bottom, and then on along a track rising through a break in the cliffs ahead, **The Heughs**. Keep going across the top to the field corner and turn through a gate on the right.

⑦ Walk away, initially beside the left-hand boundary, but after 150yds (137m), by a gate, bear right to follow the line of the ridge higher up. Eventually meeting the corner of a wall, continue ahead beside it. Shortly after crossing a track, go on over a stile, beyond which the path becomes more enclosed. Approaching the village, the path turns abruptly left behind a house and emerges on to a street. Follow it down to the main lane and turn right, back to the car park.

> **WHERE TO EAT AND DRINK** ⓘ
>
> It's not easy to resist the pervasive aroma of the **smokehouse**, where a small restaurant serves, not only kippers, but other local delicacies too. Alternatively, try the village pub, the **Jolly Fisherman**, well-respected and especially famous for its crab sandwiches. The **café** by the car park is also conveniently sited for a range of hot and cold snacks.

And on to a Nature Reserve

Extend the walk to old quarries, now the Arnold Memorial Nature Reserve.
See map and information panel for Walk 13

•DISTANCE•	2 miles (3.2km)
•MINIMUM TIME•	45min
•ASCENT / GRADIENT•	121ft (37m)
•LEVEL OF DIFFICULTY•	

Walk 14 Directions (Walk 13 option)

Craster evolved as a simple fishing village, prospering from once-plentiful herring shoals. It later developed a second industry that exploited the whinstone cliffs behind. The hard volcanic rock proved ideal for road-building and the stone, cut into small blocks, was used as paving setts until the advent of tarred roads, when it was then crushed into aggregate.

Quarrying ceased in the 1930s and the area has since reverted to natural scrub and woodland, harbouring a rich variety of both tree and plant species. Well sheltered, on the coast and with a stream below, it has developed into an important habitat particularly favoured by songbirds such as warblers, chiffchaff and blackcap. The thick foliage means they are not always easily seen, but their calls and songs let you know they are about.

Start by an information panel in the car park behind the tourist information centre, where a footpath is signed to Craster South Farm. It leads through the now-luxuriant woodland of the reserve at the base of the former quarries. Where the path later forks, bear left to arrive shortly at a kissing gate. Walk out of the field corner on a path that heads through a shallow gully. Keep going where the way levels above to find a kissing gate near the far corner.

Emerging on to a lane, Point Ⓐ, turn left and follow it for ¼ mile (400m) to **Howick Scar farm**, turn in beside the cottage at a sign to Craster, and walk through the yard. Keep going through gates past barns and on along a field track, rising to a break in the gorse-clad cliffs ahead, **Long Heugh**.

Emerging at the edge of rough grazing, Point Ⓑ, bear left along the top towards the corner of the enclosure and there turn right, following the boundary towards the coast. Ignore a footpath off on the left and continue down to a kissing gate in the bottom corner. The village lies only a short distance along the coast and you can keep to the low cliff top behind the houses until almost reaching the harbour. There, turn in through a small garden area behind the village pub to the street. Walk down past the **smokehouse** to the harbour and go left to return to the car park.

Above Kielder's Dam

Capture the essence of two of Britain's biggest man-made creations.

•DISTANCE•	3¼ miles (5.3km)
•MINIMUM TIME•	1hr 45min
•ASCENT / GRADIENT•	197ft (60m) ▲▲▲
•LEVEL OF DIFFICULTY•	🏃🏃 🏃🏃 🏃🏃
•PATHS•	Mostly rubble-surfaced tracks
•LANDSCAPE•	Lake surrounded by forested hills
•SUGGESTED MAP•	aqua3 OS Explorer OL42 Kielder Water & Forest
•START / FINISH•	Grid reference: NY 706883
•DOG FRIENDLINESS•	Dogs can be off lead
•PARKING•	Large car park at Hawkhope
•PUBLIC TOILETS•	At car park
•CONTRIBUTOR•	Anthony Toole

Walk 15 Directions

The most westerly limits of Northumbria are defined by the tortuous meanderings of the Scottish border. Here, where the population, already thin, reaches its lowest density, is the largest non-natural forest in Britain. And within this forest is northern Europe's largest non-natural lake.

The Percy and Swinburne families owned much of the land around the valley of the River North Tyne and the Percys built Kielder Castle as a shooting lodge in 1775. During the 19th century, coal was mined on land now submerged by the reservoir. Some was used locally, while a good proportion was carried, by packhorse and later by railway, for sale across the border.

By the mid-1930s, mining had come to an end, but was set to be replaced by a new industry. In 1919, the Forestry Commission was formed to cater for Britain's timber needs. In 1924 it bought 2,000 acres (810ha) near Falstone and, in 1932, a further 47,000 acres (19,035ha). Following World War Two, more land was acquired and planting extended. To house the workers needed for this rapidly expanding enterprise, forestry villages were built at Kielder, in the centre of the forest, and at Byrness and Stonehaugh near its eastern edges.

The various plantations that are now linked together to make up Kielder Forest cover a total area of 100,000 acres (40,500ha). The trees are made up almost entirely of five conifer species: Norway and sitka spruce, Scots and lodgepole pine

> ### WHAT TO LOOK FOR ℹ
> The best viewpoint on this walk is from the top of the **Belling Crag**, which juts out over the lake shore. The crag is made of fell sandstone and was once an important rock climbing venue, with about two dozen routes on its steep faces. However, because of the construction of the reservoir, climbing is no longer possible here.

Walk 15

and Japanese larch. Kielder Castle is now the administrative headquarters of Forest Enterprise, and also houses a visitors' information centre.

In 1974, the order was made authorising the construction of Kielder Reservoir, to provide water for the cities and industries of the north east. Work began in 1975 and was completed five years later. In December 1980, Kielder Water began to fill up, and the scheme was officially opened in May 1982.

WHERE TO EAT AND DRINK ⓘ

A good selection of meals is available at the **Watersedge Restaurant** at Tower Knowe Visitors' Centre. You can dine while enjoying a mesmerising view of the lake and forest through picture windows.

The dam is ¾ mile (1.2km) long and 170ft (52m) high. The shoreline encloses a lake 7 miles (11.3km) in length and has a capacity of 44 billion gallons (200 billion litres). Water is released through the valve tower, which rises from the lake 190yds (174m) from the dam. It flows into the North Tyne and from there to the Tyne. Some of the water is extracted at Riding Mill and pumped through a tunnel under the Durham moors into the Wear and the Tees.

Controversy generated by the building of the reservoir has been silenced by the lake's recreational value and its undoubted enhancement of the scenery of the North Tyne Valley.

From the western end of Hawkhope car park, take the north shore footpath through the trees and on to the rubble-covered forest road. Follow this to the left. After 100yds

(91m), go down the track on the left to the lake shore. This track zig-zags, generally parallel to the shoreline, over a small footbridge and past the remains of a **bastle** (fortified farm building). Follow the wooden waymarkers round an inlet of the lake and over two footbridges to the furthest reach of the inlet.

Follow the track on the left, which leads across a narrow isthmus on to the Belling peninsula. At a fork in the track, go right and continue around the shore of **The Belling**. There are excellent views across the lake from several points and at one viewpoint there is a reconstruction of a corbelled beehive hut.

After re-crossing the isthmus, you come to a fork in the track. Follow the left fork uphill to a junction with a larger track and turn left at a ruined sheep pen. This track leads, in 110yds (100m) back on to the main forest road. Follow this to the left, gently uphill. From the upper levels of the road, where the forest has been cleared, there are views of the lake and one of its larger inlets.

WHILE YOU'RE THERE ⓘ

Near the southern end of the dam, a track of ½ mile (800m) leads uphill to **Falstone Moss**. This is a small nature reserve and Site of Special Scientific Interest, and is the most accessible of a number of similar sites in Kielder Forest, known as the Border Mires.

At the highest point, turn right on to a partly overgrown track. Follow this for 1½ miles (2.4km) until you come to a rubble track at **High Hawkhope**. Turn right and, after a few hundred paces, right again. Continue to the dam, which is now clearly visible in front of you. The car park lies just beyond the dam.

Walk 16

Otterburn's Battlefields

Skirt a medieval battlefield and a training ground for modern warriors.

•DISTANCE•	4½ miles (7.2km)
•MINIMUM TIME•	2hrs
•ASCENT / GRADIENT•	300ft (91m)
•LEVEL OF DIFFICULTY•	
•PATHS•	Bridleway, moorland track and metalled road
•LANDSCAPE•	Open moorland with extensive views
•SUGGESTED MAP•	aqua3 OS Explorer OL42 Kielder Water & Forest
•START / FINISH•	Grid reference: NY 889929
•DOG FRIENDLINESS•	Keep on lead on roads and near sheep
•PARKING•	Roadside car park at eastern end of Otterburn village
•PUBLIC TOILETS•	Beside bridge in Otterburn
•NOTE•	Close to MOD danger area. When red flags flying, walk may be inadvisable. Contact Range Control Officer on 01830 520569 or 0191 239 4261
•CONTRIBUTOR•	Anthony Toole

BACKGROUND TO THE WALK

Until the mid-19th century, Otterburn was a hamlet hidden away in the Northumbrian moors. The main coach route from London to Edinburgh passed through Wooler and Coldstream. By 1841, the Newcastle to Jedburgh road had been extended to Edinburgh, and Otterburn became an important staging post on that route.

The Battle of Otterburn

The fame of Otterburn, however, rests on the battle fought there in 1388. This period was characterised by unrest along the Scottish border and frequent incursions by both English and Scots. In response to an invasion by the English three years earlier, a force of some 50,000 Scottish soldiers crossed the border in two divisions. The main force crossed near Carlisle. A smaller, diversionary force, of 300 cavalry and 2,000 foot soldiers, under the earls of Douglas, Moray and Dunbar, attacked through Northumberland.

Having reached as far south as Durham, the eastern division, laden with plunder, returned north. At Newcastle, they engaged in a series of skirmishes with a force led by the Earl of Northumberland's son, Sir Henry Percy, knicknamed Hotspur because of his lightning raids against the Scots. During one of these encounters, Douglas captured Hotspur's pennant and threatened to raise it on his own castle.

Harry Hotspur

To avenge this gross insult, Hotspur pursued Douglas northward and caught up with him at Otterburn. Heavily outnumbering the Scots, Percy attacked their position on the moonlit night of 19 August. During the battle, Douglas was mortally wounded, but the Scots fought so well that Percy was captured and held to ransom. An estimated 100 Scots were killed compared with more than 1,000 English.

Otterburn became known as the battle that was won by a dead man. It inspired the ballad *Chevy Chase*, one of the earliest poems in the English language. Harry Hotspur, together with his father and brother helped depose Richard II and replace him with Henry IV. He later turned against the King, and died at the battle of Shrewsbury in 1403. He is also a character in Shakespeare's plays, *Richard II* and *Henry IV*.

Today's Warriors
Modern warfare also finds a place at Otterburn. In 1911, the War Office bought 19,000 acres (7,695ha) of land to the north for use as an artillery range. The Otterburn Training Area was extended during World War Two and now covers 58,000 acres (23,490ha), about one fifth of the total area of the Northumberland National Park. It is the largest firing range in the UK.

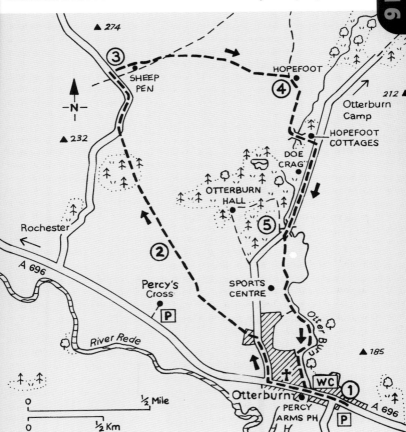

Walk 16 Directions

① From the car park, walk through **Otterburn**. About 100yds (91m) after passing the **Church of St John the Evangelist**, turn right on to the road to Otterburn Hall. At the top of the incline, go on to the public bridleway on the left, past farm buildings and into a field. Follow the bridleway alongside the wall and through a gate into the next field. Continue, this time with the wall, which gives way to a wire fence, on your right.

Walk 16

② Go through the next gate and, keeping in the same direction, cross the field to a gate through the opposite wall. Go through the gate and across marshy ground past a small plantation, now mostly cut down, to a junction with a metalled road. Follow this to the right, across a cattle grid and around the bend to the left, up a gentle incline.

③ About 100yds (91m) after the bend, follow a grassy track across the hillside to the right, past a sheep pen. This leads to a gate, beyond which is a military warning notice. Go through the gate and continue across moorland, gently downhill. The ground is boggy and the track indefinite in places, but it leads to a better track which follows a fence on your right to join a metalled road at **Hopefoot farm**.

④ Follow the road to the right, crossing a bridge over the stream, then through woods, to join the main army camp to Otterburn road at **Hopefoot Cottages**. Turn right

and follow the road past **Doe Crag cottages** and across a bridge to the entrance to **Otterburn Hall**. Go through the gate opposite this on to a footpath, signposted to Otterburn and leading across a field.

⑤ Follow the track, passing a sports centre on your right. At a bend in the wire fence, the track forks. Follow the left fork downhill, across two small footbridges, through a kissing gate and along the river bank. The track may be muddy and overgrown at times. After crossing a stile, the track brings you into **Otterburn**, just opposite the **Percy Arms**. Turn left and return to the car park.

Walk 17

The Ancient Spirit of the Simonsides

A hill that had religious significance to early settlers and is now a rock climbers' playground.

•DISTANCE•	5½ miles (8.8km)
•MINIMUM TIME•	3hrs
•ASCENT / GRADIENT•	820ft (250m)
•LEVEL OF DIFFICULTY•	
•PATHS•	Generally good tracks, but steep and muddy in places
•LANDSCAPE•	Forest, hill and moorland
•SUGGESTED MAP•	aqua3 OS Explorer OL42 Kielder Water & Forest
•START / FINISH•	Grid reference: NZ 037997
•DOG FRIENDLINESS•	Can be off lead
•PARKING•	Large car park at forest picnic area
•PUBLIC TOILETS•	None on route
•CONTRIBUTOR•	Anthony Toole

BACKGROUND TO THE WALK

While the Simonside Hills are not the highest in Northumberland, they are the most distinctive. The taller Cheviots and hills of the North Pennines present a rounded, soft face to the visitor, so that it is often difficult from a distance, to distinguish one from another. In contrast, the summit plateau of Simonside, with its chopped-off, craggy edges is recognisable from as far south as Newcastle and parts of County Durham.

Fell Sandstones

The rocks that give these hills their appearance are geologically among the youngest in the county. They consist of fell sandstones, deposited as river sediments on top of the older shale, limestone and volcanic layers that form the bedrock. Although they are exposed elsewhere in Northumberland, nowhere are they as impressive as they are on Simonside.

Craggy Summits

The cragbound summits, wrapped in a sombre, almost watchful atmosphere, have influenced people for as long as the surrounding land has been inhabited. The sandstones have proved soft enough for early settlers to leave their mark, yet hard enough for these marks to survive relentless weathering for 5,000 years. Throughout this time, agriculture was carried out in the valleys and across the lower slopes, but not on Simonside itself, suggesting that to generations of peoples it may have held some spiritual significance.

Ancient Sites

At many sites, most notably Lordenshaws, where the Simonside ridge tails off to the roadside, a record of human activity for the whole of this period has been preserved. Many of the rocks show 'cup and ring' carvings dating from neolithic times. The Bronze Age is represented by 4,000-year-old cairns and burial mounds, while the top of the hill is dominated by an Iron-Age earthwork built around 350 BC. More recent remains, dating back only a few centuries include walls, old tracks and the spoil heaps of 19th-century lead prospecting.

Scaling the Heights

Conifer forests now cover the lower reaches of these hills, but the summit crags remain clear, to be used for an activity that many of its devotees regard as a modern spiritual pursuit. As a sport, rock climbing began in Northumberland in the late 19th century, very soon after its birth in the Lake District and Snowdonia. The early pioneers included Sir Charles Trevelyan and the historian, G M Trevelyan from nearby Wallington Hall. The crags of Simonside were among the first to be developed and are still used extensively. The forest has rendered some rock faces temporarily invisible and others less accessible than hitherto, but the crags of the northern rim of Simonside are among the most popular in the county.

Walk 17 Directions

① From the notice board in the picnic area, go through the gate on to the broad forest road. Follow this gently uphill, swinging to the right round the long hairpin bend, then back left at the top of the hill. When the road splits, take the right-hand fork, past the **communications mast** and go gently downhill. When you get to the next junction, take the left-hand fork and follow the road past the sign indicating a detour to **Little Church Rock**.

> ### WHERE TO EAT AND DRINK ⓘ
> The **Queen's Head Hotel** on Rothbury's main street serves meals and welcomes children, as does the **Railway Hotel** by the bridge over the River Coquet on the Simonside road. For light refreshments, **Harley's Tea Room and Restaurant** opposite the Railway Hotel is quiet, child-friendly and gives very good service.

② When you come to the marker post, where a narrow track leads to the left, ignore this and continue along the broad track, which now becomes grassy. After passing a huge, heavily overgrown boulder, continue to the small **cairn** which marks the start of a subsidiary track on the left. Follow this track uphill through the forest and out on to the heather-covered hillside. You will now see Simonside's crags ½ mile (800m) away to your left.

③ Continue up the narrow track to join the broader one at the edge of the upper forest and follow this for about 275yds (251m) to the corner of the trees. A rough track, sometimes quite muddy in places, picks its way through boulders up the hillside. Follow this, keeping the crags on your left-hand side, on to

the plateau and walk along the top of the crags to the large **cairn** on the summit, which is probably a burial mound.

④ Away from the summit, the track splits into two. Follow the right fork across boggy ground for ⅓ mile (530m). Climb the short rise keeping the wonderfully wind-sculpted **Old Stell Crag** to your left and move round on to the summit and another large **cairn**.

> ### WHILE YOU'RE THERE ⓘ
> At Great Tosson, on the road from Rothbury to Simonside, is the ruined **Tosson Tower**, built 600 years ago by the Ogle family as a defence against the marauding reivers. A few hundred paces along the road from Great Tosson to Little Tosson you'll find one of the best-preserved 19th-century **lime kilns** in Northumberland.

⑤ Take the narrow path down to join the lower track. This leads, in ½ mile (800m), to the cairn on **Dove Crag**. At the Y-junction, ¼ mile (400m) further on, follow the right fork gently uphill to **The Beacon cairn**, and continue downhill for ½ mile (800m) to join the road at Lordenshaws car park.

⑥ Turn left and follow the road for 1 mile (1.6km) until you arrive back at the forest picnic area at the start of the walk.

> ### WHAT TO LOOK FOR ⓘ
> The detour to **Little Church Rock** is only about 120yds (110m). The smooth, rounded architecture of the rock is the result of wind erosion. The surface ripple effect is caused by softer rock being eroded more than harder layers. Look for Stone-Age cup markings near the bottom of the rock.

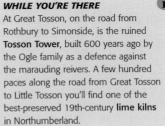

Walk 18

Elsdon, Heart of Reiver Country

A once-lawless landscape of rolling hills and valleys, with one of Northumberland's most interesting villages.

•DISTANCE•	4 miles (6.4km)
•MINIMUM TIME•	1hr 45min
•ASCENT / GRADIENT•	623ft (190m) ▲▲▲
•LEVEL OF DIFFICULTY•	🚶🚶 🚶🚶 🚶🚶
•PATHS•	Field paths and tracks
•LANDSCAPE•	Rolling farmland surrounding village of Elsdon
•SUGGESTED MAP•	aqua3 OS Explorer OL42 Keilder Water & Forest
•START / FINISH•	Grid reference: NY 937932
•DOG FRIENDLINESS•	Dogs on leads
•PARKING•	Signed car park in Elsdon, by bridge on Rothbury road
•PUBLIC TOILETS•	In village hall at start of walk
•CONTRIBUTOR•	David Winpenny

BACKGROUND TO THE WALK

For hundreds of years in the Middle Ages, Elsdon was at the centre of some of the most lawless land in England. It was the capital of the remote Middle March – one of three Marches or protective areas set up in 1249 to protect the border lands. Local historian G M Trevelyan wrote that Elsdon was 'the capital of Redesdale when neither Scotland nor England existed.' The chief threat to the area was from the reivers or mosstroopers – bands of marauders, mostly from north of the border, who carried out raids on local farms, burning the crops, destroying homesteads and, above all, stealing cattle, sheep and horses. Such was the seriousness of these raids that they influenced the design of the village. Its wide green, more than 7 acres (2.8ha) in area, was used to pen animals during a raid, and the entrances to the village were shut off.

Tower and Castle

Another important reminder of those anarchistic days is the Vicar's Pele at Elsdon, just by the church. A square, defensive tower that could be easily defended, it was probably built in the 14th century, and rebuilt in the 16th and 18th. Its walls are up to 9ft (3m) thick. Lewis Carroll's grandfather, later the Bishop of Ossory, lived in the tower from 1762 to 1765.

The remains of earlier defences are a highlight of the first part of the walk. What are known locally as Mote Hills are the spectacular remains of a motte and bailey castle. Sitting on the steep banks of Elsdon Burn the castle has a lower area – the bailey – surrounded by a deep ditch and bank, while the tall hill behind – the motte – once supported a timber castle. Put up by the de Umfravilles in the 12th century, Elsdon Castle had a short life – in around 1160 the family moved its headquarters to Harbottle, and left Elsdon to slumber.

The walk takes you from the village to the tiny farming hamlet of Hudspeth, which shares its name with a county in Texas, and up the slopes of Landshot Hill before descending to the hamlet of Landshot and on to the farms of East and West Todholes. From

Elizabethan county records we know that in January 1582 Thomas Routledge of Todholes issued a complaint against Kinmont Armstrong of Canonbie, in Galloway, who he claimed had stolen '40 kine, 20 sheep, and 1 horse, value 300 pounds sterling' in a reivers raid.

Follow the Medieval Wall
The return to Elsdon, which offers good views of the village and the Mote Hills, is partially along a decayed medieval stone wall, once part of the outlying village defences. Look out, back on the Green, for the figure of Bacchus above the door of one of the cottages, which was originally an inn.

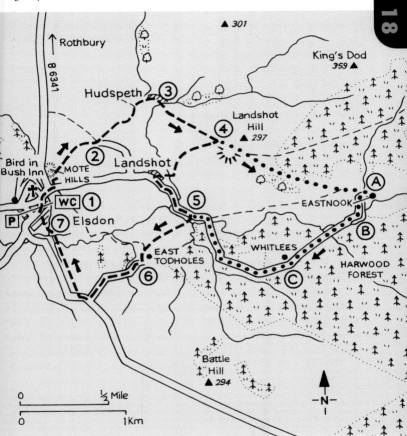

Walk 18 Directions

① Follow the 'Toilets' sign past the village hall and through a gateway. Climb the lane past the **Mote Hills**, pass the house and cross gravel to a gate. Cross the small field and go through the next gate, then head half right to go through a gate near some trees. Follow the path up a sunken lane then along the field edge to a gate.

② Go through the gate and turn left over a cattle grid. Follow the metalled lane through farm buildings and down to a row of

Walk 18

cottages. Opposite them, turn right in front of a barn, cross a stream and go through a gate.

③ Walk ahead through the field with a bank on your left and, at the top of the rise, bear left across the bank, making for a gate in a crossing wire fence. After the gate, bear half left again, towards the left-hand end of a crossing wall.

④ Turn right and follow the wall downhill. Go through a gate in a crossing wall and continue to follow the wall on your left to reach a waymarked post. Turn right, cross a small bridge, then go uphill to a gate beside a barn. Go straight on, then take a metal gate on your left. Curve right to another gate on to a road. Turn left along the road, crossing a cattle grid and a bridge, to a second cattle grid.

⑤ Cross the cattle grid, then turn immediately right, signed 'East Todholes'. Cross the stream and go through a gate, then cross a second stream. Follow the wall on your left-hand side to reach a ladder stile by pine trees. After the stile bear half left to go round the right-hand side of **East Todholes farm** and cross over a stile on to a lane.

⑥ Follow the lane past the next farm and up the hill to join a road. Turn right. Opposite the 'bend' sign go right over a stile. Follow the old wall downhill towards **Elsdon**, bending right, then left, at a fence to go over a stile. After another stile bear right to a footbridge, then left to another. The path eventually brings you to larger footbridge near the village.

⑦ Cross the footbridge, then turn right to a stile beside a gate. Go up the track between some houses to a road that takes you to the green. Bear right, along the edge of the green, go over the bridge and back to the start.

Walk 19

Eastnook and Whitlees

An extension that takes you into the edge of the vast Harwood Forest.
See map and information panel for Walk 18

•DISTANCE•	6 miles (9.7km)
•MINIMUM TIME•	2hrs 15min
•ASCENT / GRADIENT•	787ft (240m) ▲▲ ▲▲ ▲
•LEVEL OF DIFFICULTY•	🚶 🚶 🚶

Walk 19 Directions (Walk 18 option)

At Point ④ on the main walk, turn left over the stile and continue with the wall on your right. There are wide views of Redesdale from this section of the walk. After about ¼ mile (400m) turn right to go over a ladder stile, then bear left across the field towards the corner of the plantation ahead.

WHAT TO LOOK FOR ⓘ
The **Emperor moth** has been seen on the moorland around Whitlees. You may spot the brown, woolly caterpillars which turn bright green with bands of black as they get older. The female adult moth has grey wings with a spot like an eye on each wing which it uses to startle would-be predators.

Go over the wall on a waymarked stile. Keeping the trees to your left, pass a waymarked post. Cross a wall at a stone stile and head straight across the field in the direction of **Eastnook farm**, behind the trees. Pass a waymarked post and go over a stone stile. Continue ahead down the field, in line with the telegraph poles, and over another stile on to a narrow lane (Point Ⓐ).

Turn right, down the road, and follow it through a metal gate into **Harwood Forest** (Point Ⓑ) This huge plantation of sitka spruce and lodgepole pine was planted in the 1950s on the sandstone of the Simonside Hills. In the open areas you may see purple moor-grass, sheep's fescue, wavy hair-grass and soft rush, as well as heather. Don't be surprised if you see a wheeled sledge pulled by huskies in the forest: the Siberian Husky Club uses it for competitions.

The lane passes the houses at **Whitlees** (Point Ⓒ). Near by is a bastle house – a fortified farmstead – probably dating from the 16th century. It is built of very large rough stones, and seems to have had a ground floor, where animals were kept, and a low upper living floor. When built, it would have been sited on the open moorland. Follow the lane through a gateway and past farm building to the cattle grid at Point ⑤ on the main walk.

WHILE YOU'RE THERE ⓘ
Visit **Harbottle Castle**, just across the moors. The de Umfravilles moved here from Elsdon. It has fine earthworks, and the remains of part of the 13th-century curtain wall. The keep was rebuilt in 1545 and you can still see some of the oval gun loops in them.

Remarkable Cragside

A walk around the creation of a Victorian industrial genius.

Walk 20

•DISTANCE•	3 miles (4.8km)
•MINIMUM TIME•	2hrs
•ASCENT / GRADIENT•	492ft (150m) ▲▲ ▲▲
•LEVEL OF DIFFICULTY•	🚶🚶 🚶🚶 🚶
•PATHS•	Well-marked tracks, occasionally muddy
•LANDSCAPE•	Man-made forest and gardens on steep hillside
•SUGGESTED MAP•	aqua3 OS Explorer 332 Alnwick & Amble or free map from visitors' centre (clearer)
•START / FINISH•	Grid reference: NU 071026
•DOG FRIENDLINESS•	Dogs allowed on paths but not into formal gardens
•PARKING•	Large car park near visitors' centre
•PUBLIC TOILETS•	At visitors' centre and at play area
•NOTE•	National Trust Cragside Estate usually open April–December
•CONTRIBUTOR•	Anthony Toole

Walk 20 Directions

William George Armstrong (1810–1900) was born in Newcastle. He trained as a solicitor, but found his main interests lay in science and engineering. In 1842, he constructed a hydro-electric generator and four years later, began to develop hydraulic cranes. This business was so successful that he abandoned his law practice to build a factory at Elswick, on the banks of the Tyne. In the 1850s, after the Crimean War, Armstrong devoted much of his efforts to armaments, and his factories supplied armies and navies across the world. During the American

WHAT TO LOOK FOR ℹ
The **Pump House** and **Power House** are open to visitors and contain replicas of Armstrong's machinery. Many of the trees in the Pinetum, between the iron bridge and the Power House, have plaques to aid in their identification.

Civil War, both sides were equipped with Armstrong's weaponry. Machinery for Tyneside's shipbuilding was made at Elswick, as was the mechanism for raising London's Tower Bridge.

The legacy of Lord Armstrong, as he later became, can be seen all over the north east. The waterwheel at Killhope Lead Mining Centre in County Durham, and the hydraulic engine to be seen at Allenheads were made at the Elswick factory. Jesmond Dene, in Newcastle, was home to Lord and Lady Armstrong, and its landscaping is thought to have provided much of the inspiration for their later work at Cragside. Jesmond Dene was gifted to the City of Newcastle in 1883.

In their later years, the Armstrongs channelled their energies into Cragside House and Estate. The house was designed by Richard Norman Shaw and built using local sandstone. Two lakes were created

Walk 20

and their waters used to generate electricity, which powered the house. Cragside was the first house in the world to be lit by hydro-electricity. The inventor of the incandescent light bulb, Joseph Swan, was a friend of Lord Armstrong. The house had hot and cold running water, central heating, telephones and a service lift from the kitchen.

The grounds were the preserve of Lady Margaret Armstrong, who was a keen botanist. She designed the rock gardens and nurtured exotic plants from around the world in glasshouses and the Orchard House. The hillside was planted with 7 million trees and bushes to create a 1,000-acre (404ha) forest. Again, these were imported from America, Japan and Africa, and include the tallest Douglas fir in England. The Cragside Estate is now owned by the National Trust and isn't open all year round, so check before you set out.

From the visitors' centre, follow the sign to the **Armstrong Trail**. The dam and **Tumbleton Lake** are on your right. Cross the road and continue to the **Pump House**. Cross the footbridge and turn left, following the sign to the Power House. The trail leads through thick woodland, crossing the river twice to a point that gives a marvellous view of the house. Keep following signs to the Power House, past the **Iron Bridge** and zig-zagging along the hillside, over footbridges and down to a waterwheel. Turn right to the **Power House**.

Return to the wheel and follow signs uphill to reach the house (**Cragside**). Turn sharp right on to a metalled road labelled Estate Drive. After 25yds (23m), follow a stepped path signposted to the tarn. At a junction, go right, and continue through a natural tunnel of sandstone boulders, then left where the track forks to the tarn. Where trees have been cleared, there are views over the Coquet and Rothbury to the Simonside Hills.

WHERE TO EAT AND DRINK ⓘ
The **restaurant** at the visitors' centre serves meals, teas and ice creams as well as home-made Victorian and regional recipes. This was once the stable block and has a courtyard with tables for dining outdoors in good weather.

Follow the track to the viewpoint and lakes, uphill past a wonderful array of sandstone crags. At a T-junction, turn right then, where the road forks, go left and after 220yds (201m) reach the play area. Go through this on to the road and turn right. Just before the bridge, turn left on to the track that leads round the side of **Nelly's Moss Lakes**. Near the northern end of the second lake, after crossing a bridge, turn left. Just before the second bridge, follow a fork to the right. This track leads alongside a stream and past the water boxes of the timber flume. Go uphill to join the main drive at Canada car park.

Go right along the road to Moorside car park, with views over the heather moorlands. From the back of the car park, follow the track signposted to **Canada Drive**. On reaching this, turn right and follow signposts to the house. At a crossroads, take the track to the right, down a steep staircase, and straight across at the next crossroads on to the track above the house. Turn right and return to the car park and **visitors' centre**.

Around Druridge Bay

A nature reserve, country park and beach, each with its own interest.

•DISTANCE•	5½ miles (8.8km)
•MINIMUM TIME•	1hr 45min
•ASCENT / GRADIENT•	Negligible
•LEVEL OF DIFFICULTY•	
•PATHS•	Paths and tracks, with good walk on beach, no stiles
•LANDSCAPE•	Dunes, seashore and lakeside
•SUGGESTED MAP•	aqua3 OS Explorers 325 Morpeth & Blyth; 332 Alnwick & Amble
•START / FINISH•	Grid reference: NU 282024 (on Explorer 332)
•DOG FRIENDLINESS•	On lead within nature reserve
•PARKING•	Car park at Hauxley Nature Reserve
•PUBLIC TOILETS•	At Hauxley Nature Reserve and Druridge Bay Country Park visitor centres
•NOTE•	Check tides; complete coastal section not always passable at high water
•CONTRIBUTOR•	Dennis Kelsall

BACKGROUND TO THE WALK

The story of Druridge Bay's pools begins 300 millions years ago, when the area basked in a warm climate and was cloaked in a dense, forest swamp. The gradual accumulation of decaying vegetation eventually gave rise to extensive coal deposits, which today extend far out to sea. Although dug from shallow drifts or bell pits since the medieval period, it was only during the Industrial Revolution that coal mining began in earnest. Pits were sunk ever deeper, and mining developed as a major industry along the north east coast, with villages such as nearby Broomhill springing up to house miners and their families.

Opencast Mining

As the 20th century progressed, many pits became worked out or uneconomic, yet with the Second World War, the need for coal had never been greater. A new approach was tried, with the country's first opencast operation beginning on Town Moor near Newcastle. Far cheaper and simpler than deep mining, the scale of workings steadily increased, as the equipment needed to excavate and move immense quantities of rock was improved.

Work began on the Radcliffe site in September 1971, and a staggering 100 million tons of overlying rock was removed to extract some 2½ million tons of coal. Within seven years, all the coal was out, leaving behind a crater 170ft (52m) deep. The Northumberland Wildlife Trust bought part of the site in 1983 and has turned the derelict wasteland into the nature-rich lakes and islands we see today.

Nature Reserves

Hauxley Pool is typical of the several flooded workings along the coast, and although huge numbers of trees, shrubs and other plants were originally brought in, there is now a remarkably natural feel to the water and its surroundings. As the fertility of the once-barren land has been improved, many species have become established on the banks and, in spring and summer, the place is alive with colour from bloody cranesbill, yellow wort, kidney vetch and a host of other flowers. Look carefully and you'll spot the delicate pink petals of ragged robin, an often-rare sight in today's countryside.

The attraction for many visitors, however, is the variety and numbers of birds that visit these coastal lakes, a spectacle that is ever-changing throughout the year. Resident populations are joined by those migrating between the summer feeding and breeding grounds in the far north and the warmer climes of Africa, where many spend the winter. Dunlin, whimbrel and sanderling are amongst the many species passing through, whilst redshank, plover and bar-tailed godwit are some that winter here. You will also see whooper and Bewick swans as well as many favourites such as tits, finches, blackbirds and robins.

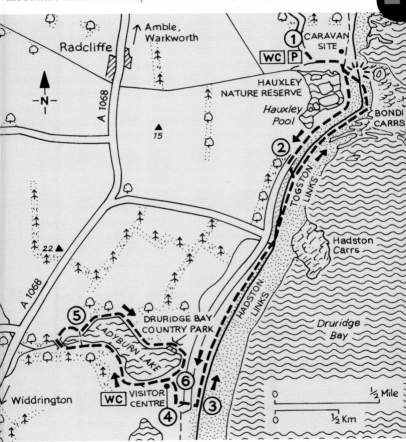

Walk 21 Directions

① A waymarked footpath beside the car park entrance winds between the nature reserve and a caravan site towards the coast.

Through a gate at the bottom, turn right on to a track, which shortly passes two gates that give access to bird hides overlooking the lake.

② Leaving the reserve, continue a little further along a tarmac track to

Walk 21

an informal parking area on the left, where there is easy access on to the beach. Now, follow the shore past **Togston Links**, across a stream and on below **Hadston Links**.

③ After 1¼ miles (2km), wooden steps take the path off the sands on to the dunes. Cross a tarmac track and continue over a marshy area into pinewood. Beyond the trees, emerge by a car park and walk across to the **Druridge Bay Country Park visitor centre**, where there is a café and toilets.

④ A footway to the left winds around **Ladyburn Lake**, soon passing a boat launching area. Keep to the lower path, which soon leads to stepping stones across the upper neck of the lake. If you would rather not cross there, continue around the upper edge of a wooded nature sanctuary above the water to a footbridge higher up. Over the bridge and through a gate, turn

right by the field edge, soon dropping around an internal corner to a kissing gate. Descend through trees to regain the lake by the stepping stones.

⑤ This side of the lake has a more 'natural' feel, the path winding through trees to emerge beside a lushly vegetated shoreline where swans like to feed. After crossing a bridge over the lake's outflow, carry on back to the visitor centre.

⑥ Retrace your steps to the beach and turn back towards **Hauxley**, but when you reach the point at which you originally dropped on to the sands, remain on the shore towards **Bondi Carrs**. Seaweed can make the rocks slippery, so be careful clambering over as you round the point, where Coquet Island then comes into view ahead. Not far beyond there, after passing a look-out post and approaching large rocks placed as a storm defence, leave across the dunes, retracing your outward path the short distance back to the car park.

Morpeth and its River

Below Morpeth lies a fine woodland valley walk.

•DISTANCE•	8½ miles (13.7km)
•MINIMUM TIME•	2hrs 45min
•ASCENT / GRADIENT•	420ft (128m)
•LEVEL OF DIFFICULTY•	
•PATHS•	Woodland paths (muddy after rain) and field paths, 9 stiles
•LANDSCAPE•	Wooded valley, attractive park
•SUGGESTED MAP•	aqua3 OS Explorer 325 Morpeth & Blyth
•START / FINISH•	Grid reference: NZ 198859
•DOG FRIENDLINESS•	On lead through town and on roads
•PARKING•	Car parks within town
•PUBLIC TOILETS•	Signed in town
•CONTRIBUTOR•	Dennis Kelsall

BACKGROUND TO THE WALK

The 16th-century travel writer, John Leland, described Morpeth as a 'fayrer towne than Alnwicke', a sentiment still upheld by the town's natives. It certainly is an attractive place, with many streets lined by fine Georgian buildings and a sprinkling of some that are considerably older. But it isn't a museum either, and its work-a-day bustle reflects a long tradition as a market town, just over 800 years in fact. This walk leads you past some of its most interesting sights, but there are others too, which are worth wandering to.

The Early Days

Little remains of the town's original buildings, which witnessed the often bloody events that marked its early history as a frontier town. Fortified shortly after the Norman Conquest, the first defence was a motte and bailey surmounting a mound, Ha Hill, overlooking the river in what is now Carlisle Park. This was superseded by more sophisticated fortifications on the higher ground behind, of which the 14th-century gatehouse still survives. The town had an abbey too, founded a little way upstream as a daughter to the great Cistercian monastery at Fountains. The medieval looking 'castle' opposite the park entrance, however, only appeared in 1821, serving successively as the gaol, police headquarters and then courthouse before being converted to residential use.

The old town bridge was replaced in 1832, its passage so narrow that, on two occasions, the mail coach crashed through the parapets to meet an untimely and watery end. It was replaced by Thomas Telford's graceful three-arched span, which, before the bypass was built, carried the Great North Road. At its northern end stands the Chantry, built in the late 13th century to serve as a chapel and tollhouse for the original bridge. Its chaplain began the town's first grammar school, which, refounded after the Chantry was dissolved along with the monastery by Henry VIII, continued in the building until 1858, when it moved to Cottingwood. The elegant Town Hall, gifted in 1714 by the Earl of Carlisle and re-fronted by Lord Joicey two centuries later, stands near the clock tower, which dates from around 1640 and served as the town gaol until the beginning of the 19th century. From its bells, the nightly curfew was rung at 8 o'clock.

Walk 22

Morpeth has associations with many notable people, including Vice-Admiral Lord Collingwood, Nelson's second in command at Trafalgar, and Dr John Horsley, dubbed the 'Father of British Archaeology' and minister of St George's Church for 23 years. Laid to rest in St Mary's churchyard, just south of the town, is Emily Davison, one of the suffragette movement's most determined activists. Repeatedly imprisoned for her defiant protests, Davison became a martyr in 1917 when she fell beneath the King's racehorse, Anmer.

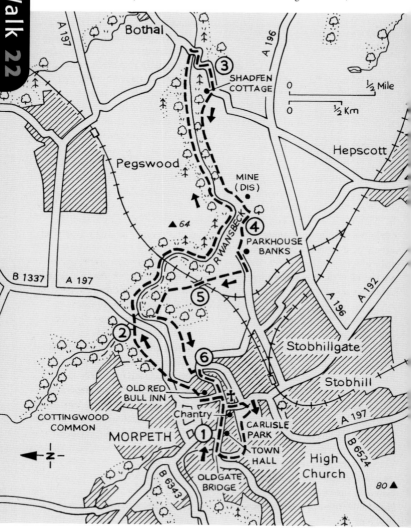

Walk 22 **Directions**

① From the Town Hall, walk east along **Bridge Street** to the end, continuing around to the left along the main road towards Pegswood. Immediately after the **Old Red Bull Inn**, take an enclosed path on the right that later rejoins the main road. Cross to a footpath rising through the woodland opposite,

Walk 22

signed 'Whorral Bank and Cottingwood Common'. Bear right when you get to a fork, past a residential home, and then go right at the next junction to again meet the main road.

② On the far side, a path, signed 'Bothal', descends into a lushly wooded valley through which flows the **River Wansbeck**. There follows a delightful, undulating walk for some 2¼ miles (3.6km), eventually ending over a stile by a sawmill. Walk to the lane beyond and turn right across the river.

③ After climbing from the valley, the lane continues above the wood. Where it later bends sharply left at **Shadfen Cottage**, go ahead over a stile into a field corner, and carry on at the edge of successive fields beside the right-hand boundary. Eventually, the way passes right of a deep excavation, once an opencast coal mine, before falling towards a stile into woodland. Drop through the trees to a bridge over a stream.

④ Re-emerging into open fields above the far bank, follow a path ahead between the cultivation to gain a tarmac track past **Parkhouse Banks**. After 120yds (110m), immediately beyond a drive, turn through a gap in the right-hand hedge, signed 'Whorral Bank', and walk away beside the field edge. At the corner, slip right through another gap and carry on along a track past a cottage and through fields to a railway bridge.

⑤ Keep going over the field beyond to a stile, there dropping across a rough pasture back into wood. Soon joined by a track, continue down to a junction by the river and turn left above the bank. Emerging from the trees, bear left along a field path that leads past a cottage, the ongoing track returning to the river.

⑥ Over the bridge, a street leads around past the ambulance station into town. Go ahead to **St George's Church** and then turn left over **Telford Bridge** to **Castle Square**. Cross into **Carlisle Park** and, beyond the flowerbeds, bear right following the main drive to a riverside promenade. Walk upstream past **Elliott Bridge** to the top of the park and there turn right over **Oldgate Bridge** to return to the town centre.

Tarset Burn and North Tyne

A once-lawless landscape of hills and valleys with an interesting village.

•DISTANCE•	7½ miles (12.1km)
•MINIMUM TIME•	3hrs
•ASCENT / GRADIENT•	1,083ft (330m) ▲▲▲
•LEVEL OF DIFFICULTY•	🚶🚶🚶
•PATHS•	Burnside and moorland paths and tracks – some wet areas
•LANDSCAPE•	Valleys with woodland and moorland
•SUGGESTED MAP•	aqua3 OS Explorer OL42 Keilder Water & Forest
•START / FINISH•	Grid reference: NY 793858
•DOG FRIENDLINESS•	Dogs on leads in farmland
•PARKING•	Beside Tarset Village Hall in Lanehead, on Greenhaugh road
•PUBLIC TOILETS•	None on route
•CONTRIBUTOR•	David Winpenny

BACKGROUND TO THE WALK

The area around Lanehead is called Tarset. The name means 'the fold in the dry pine woods' and is first recorded in the early 13th century. Although the car parking area is beside Tarset Village Hall, there is in fact no Tarset village – only the burn in its valley, a parish name and the scant and confusing remains of Tarset Castle south of Lanehead. This was started in 1267 on the site of an earlier Scottish fortress by 'Red' John Comyn, a claimant to the throne of Scotland who was stabbed to death by the altar of the Greyfriars church in Dumfries by Robert the Bruce in 1306. The castle was burned by the Scots in 1525, and largely destroyed by a railway cutting in 1860. The walk takes you alongside the Tarset Burn before crossing it and heading across moorland to Thorneyburn.

Shipshape Religion

The tiny hamlet of Thorneyburn mainly consists of the church and the large former Rectory. Both were constructed in 1818 for Greenwich Hospital. It had been given the parish after the former patron, the Earl of Derwentwater, had been disgraced for his part in the Old Pretender's rebellion of 1715. Like nearby Greystead, Wark and Humshaugh, Thorneyburn had a succession of naval chaplains as rector, and all four have very similar churches and rectories. The farmhouse at nearby Redhaugh probably started life as a fortified bastle house; at the edge of the small field opposite is a pretty pyramid-roofed 18th-century dovecote.

Disasters at Slaty Ford

Sidwood Picnic Area is the start of a number of waymarked trails though this part of the huge Kielder Forest, including the 'Reivers Trail'. As well as the ubiquitous pines there are a number of ornamental trees that remain from the old Sidwood Estate. Through the woods and over the ridge, you come to Slaty Ford – a peaceful place, but with a dark history. In September 1796 six workers in the nearby colliery shaft were killed – either by an influx of water from a disused shaft or from an explosion; the records are unclear. On 20 September 1957 a Vickers Varsity aeroplane, on a training flight from RAF Thorney Island in Sussex, crashed here, killing all five crew members.

Bridge and Railway

The beautiful suspension bridge over the River North Tyne towards the end of the walk was put up in the 1860s to provide access from the south bank to Thorneyburn Station on the Border Counties Railway. The line went from Hexham to Riccarton in the Borders, following the North Tyne Valley. It was opened in 1862 and closed in 1956. Part of the route is now submerged beneath the waters of the Kielder Reservoir.

Walk 23 **Directions**

① Walk to the staggered crossroads in the middle of **Lanehead** and turn right, signed 'Donkleywood'. At the

Redmire cottages turn right. Go through a gate, over two stiles and through a hand gate. Bear left to a stile in the field corner. Bend right, following the river bank and go over five stiles. The path rises, goes

Walk 23

through a hand gate and to a footbridge. Go through a gate at the end, then ahead to meet a track. Turn left to the farm buildings.

② Go through two gates between the buildings, then ascend the lane. As it bears left, go ahead past a waymarker and downhill to cross the stream. Pass another waymarked post and go through a gateway. Bend right after it, go through a hand gate and turn left along the fence. Go over a stile on the right, then half left towards the house and church. Keep left of a ruined wall, and then bear left to follow a wall downhill to a stream.

WHILE YOU'RE THERE ℹ
Bellingham, 3¼ miles (5.3km) east of Lanehead, has a fascinating church with a stone-vaulted roof. Outside the slightly Germanic town hall is a cannon captured during the Boxer Rebellion in China in 1900. A delightful walk from the village takes you up Hareshaw Burn gorge to Hareshaw Linn waterfall.

---

③ Cross the stream, go over the stile beyond and climb the hill. Bear left past the church to a gate. Turn right along the lane. At the T-junction turn left. Follow the lane past **Redheugh farm** and the 'Forestry Commission Sidwood' sign to **Sidwood Picnic Area**, near white-painted buildings.

④ Turn left, signed 'Slaty Ford'. Follow the path through the wood for a short distance, then take another to your right. Go over a crossing track and continue uphill. After the track levels out, it goes beside woodland to a gate. Continue through the field, winding through plantations, to cross a ford then past a signpost on to a crossing track.

⑤ Turn left and go over another ford. Continue up the track to a gate. After ¼ mile (400m) look for a stile in the wall on your right. Go over and bear half right down the field. Go over a stream, up to a wire fence and follow it left. Go right, through a gate, and cross the field, through a gate, into the farmyard.

WHERE TO EAT AND DRINK ℹ
There is nowhere directly on the route, but in nearby Greenhaugh the **Hollybush Inn** offers tea and coffee, bar snacks and dining room meals. In Bellingham there are the **Riversdale** and **Cheviot** hotels, the **Rose and Crown Inn**, **Fountain Cottage Tea Rooms** and **The Snack Bar**.

---

⑥ Take the right-hand of two gates to your left. Go through another gate and bear left to follow the track downhill. At the bottom turn left along the road. As it begins to rise, take a footpath, signed 'The Hott', over a stile. Follow the riverside path, through a kissing gate, to the suspension bridge.

⑦ Just after the hut beyond the bridge, bear left. Cross the railway embankment and go through a gate. Bear half right to a large tree in the field corner and join the road. Turn right, then bear left on the road. Continue over a cattle grid. Cross the river on a bridge and continue to **Lanehead**, turning left at the junction to the parking place.

WHAT TO LOOK FOR ℹ
Northumberland National Park is making efforts to increase and protect the **alder** tree in its area – examples have been identified near Redheugh farm. The alder has broad, dull green leaves and a black bark scarred with clefts – in winter it has greyish catkins. It thrives in marshy land, and has a deep tap root that ensures that it is fed even in drought conditions.

Black Middens

A short detour will take you to a well-preserved bastle house.
See map and information panel for Walk 23

Walk 24

•DISTANCE•	1½ miles (2.4km)
•MINIMUM TIME•	30min
•ASCENT / GRADIENT•	100ft (30m)
•LEVEL OF DIFFICULTY•	

Walk 24 **Directions** (Walk 23 option)

From Point ④ on the Walk 23, at **Sidwood Picnic Area,** continue straight on up the forest track. After ¼ mile (400m), look out below you on the right for a footbridge and go over it. Follow the forest path to another footbridge, turning right over it (Point Ⓐ).

Go through the gate at the end of the bridge and then forward along the field side. Part way along the field, bear left along the path to reach the road. Turn right along the road to reach the car park below **Black Middens Bastle House** (Point Ⓑ), and walk up the rough track to visit the ruin.

Bastles are fortified houses, restricted to the border lands. The remains of around 200 bastle houses are known, the majority of them in Northumberland. Like the others, Black Middens was built by a local farmer as protection from Scottish raids and cattle theft. With very thick walls and small windows, they were easily defended, and provide accommodation on the lower floor for beasts. Living quarters were above, originally

accessible by a ladder that could be pulled up in time of trouble – the stone steps are one of the few alterations to this 17th-century building. There are other bastle houses near Black Middens, some of which can be visited.

After visiting Black Middens, retrace your steps to the car park, back along the road and through the field to the gate on to the footbridge. Cross the bridge then turn left, signed 'Sidwood Picnic Area'. Go through a gate and follow the burn. The path eventually bears away from the burn and goes uphill. At a crossing track by the white buildings, turn left back to the open area by the picnic site. Turn right, following the 'Slaty Ford' sign, rejoining Walk 23.

WHAT TO LOOK FOR

Look out, in Bellingham churchyard, for a 700-year-old gravestone called the **Long Pack**. It is the tomb of a robber who, in 1723, was smuggled into a local house in a pedlar's pack to open the door to his accomplice. Servants saw the pack move and shot at it. The robber was killed and buried under this stone. **The Sneep**, a hillside across the Tarset Burn from Thorneyburn church, is reputed to be where King Arthur and his knights sleep, to be woken in the time of Britain's greatest need.

Newcastle and Gateshead

Newcastle is joined to go-ahead Gateshead by fine bridges over the Tyne.

Walk 25

•DISTANCE•	3 miles (4.8km)
•MINIMUM TIME•	1hr 15min
•ASCENT / GRADIENT•	131ft (40m) ▲ ▲ ▲
•LEVEL OF DIFFICULTY•	🚶 🚶 🚶
•PATHS•	Pavements and steps
•LANDSCAPE•	City centre, on banks of River Tyne
•SUGGESTED MAP•	aqua3 OS Explorer 316 Newcastle upon Tyne; AA Street-by-Street Newcastle upon Tyne
•START / FINISH•	Grid reference: NZ 258638
•DOG FRIENDLINESS•	On lead; probably not a dog's idea of fun
•PARKING•	Car park east of Baltic – the Centre for Contemporary Art
•PUBLIC TOILETS•	Baltic and several in Newcastle centre
•CONTRIBUTOR•	David Winpenny

Walk 25 Directions

From the car park, follow the quayside path beside **Baltic – the Centre for Contemporary Art** and the **Millennium Bridge** into **Baltic Square**, then bear left up steps to the road. Turn right along the road, passing beneath the **Tyne Bridge**. Symbol of Newcastle throughout the world, the semicircular bridge was built between 1925 and 1928 by Dorman Long of Middlesbrough. Further on is Robert Stephenson's High Level Bridge, with both rail and road crossings, which was completed in 1849.

At the traffic-lights, turn right and walk over the **Swing Bridge**, built by the great local engineering firm of Armstrong (▶ Walk 20). It weighs 1,450 tons and is powered by Armstrong's hydraulic engines. When it opened in 1876 it was the largest swing bridge in the world. At the end of the bridge, look right to see the half-timbered Bessie Surtees House, now cared for by English Heritage. It is a fine group of former merchants' houses and shops, rare survivors of 17th-century Newcastle.

Cross the road, bearing left, and take the steps up the hill. They go left, then emerge under an archway in front of the **castle keep**. The castle was new, and gave its name to the city, in 1080. Founded by William the Conqueror's illegitimate son, Robert Curthose, it was rebuilt 100 years later for Henry II. Inside the keep are some fine medieval chambers and a small chapel. Go round the left-hand side of the keep, and under the railway arch. The Victorians built the railway straight through the castle –

> **WHERE TO EAT AND DRINK** ⓘ
> There is no shortage of choice in Newcastle and Gateshead, from lively pubs and small cafés to grand hotels and exclusive restaurants. At the start and finish of the walk, **Baltic** has a good restaurant and a café-bar.

no wonder the Queen kept her carriage blinds down when she travelled through the city. The 13th-century Black Gate, the castle's gatehouse, is ahead. Notice the picturesque brick house, of about 1620, perched on the top.

Cross the road on your left and follow **Westgate Street**, parallel with the railway line. Continue ahead under the buildings that form an arch across the street, but look left to see the façade of Newcastle's fine railway station, a masterpiece by Newcastle architect John Dobson. By **St John's Church** on the right, turn right up **Grainger Street**. This area of Newcastle was developed by Richard Grainger in the first half of the 19th century, and has fine classically-inspired buildings. Grainger Market, with entrances on your left-hand side as you approach the Grey Monument, was the heart of his grand scheme, and is worth a visit for its impressive interior.

Follow Grainger Street as far as the **Grey Monument**. This tall column, the heart of Grainger's planning and of Newcastle, is 135ft (41m) high, and commemorates the parliamentary reformer Earl Grey. Turn right down Grey Street. Often called the finest street in Europe, it is lined with elegant classical buildings, and curves satisfyingly as

it descends. The portico of the Theatre Royal forms an excellent punctuation mark.

At **Mosley Street** turn right. At the traffic-lights, turn left by the tower of the Cathedral of St Nicholas with its rare 'crown'. Bear left, downhill, with the **Black Gate** to your right. The road descends to go under a railway arch. Continue ahead to the **Quayside**, where markets are held and much of Newcastle's pulsating nightlife is centred.

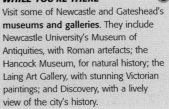

WHILE YOU'RE THERE
Visit some of Newcastle and Gateshead's **museums and galleries**. They include Newcastle University's Museum of Antiquities, with Roman artefacts; the Hancock Museum, for natural history; the Laing Art Gallery, with stunning Victorian paintings; and Discovery, with a lively view of the city's history.

Turn left and follow the Quayside as far as the **Millennium Bridge**. Opened in 2001, and winner of the Stirling Prize for Architecture in 2002, it has a unique 'blinking eye' mechanism that tilts to let ships go beneath it. Cross the bridge, then turn left, back to **Baltic**. Formerly a flour mill, this landmark building has been transformed into a centre for contemporary arts. There are observation platforms at various levels, with wonderful views over Newcastle and Gateshead.

WHAT TO LOOK FOR
The Newcastle and Gateshead area is well-served by public transport, especially with its **Metro** system, the first rapid-transit electric railway in Britain. Partly underground, and with its hub at Monument Station beneath the statue to Earl Grey at the top of Grey Street, its first section was opened in 1981. Partially using existing rail lines, tunnels and bridges (which had to be upgraded and strengthened in a massive engineering effort) it was extended first to Newcastle Airport at Woolsington and later to Washington and Sunderland. Linking with local bus services, and with stops at Newcastle Central Station, Gateshead Station and Sunderland, the Metro has 40 million passenger journeys each year. The stations are indicated by a black letter M on a yellow background.

Walk 26

Smugglers and the Light of Marsden Bay

Along the coast near South Shields, and inland to the Cleadon Hills.

•DISTANCE•	5½ miles (8.8km)
•MINIMUM TIME•	2hrs
•ASCENT / GRADIENT•	246ft (75m)
•LEVEL OF DIFFICULTY•	
•PATHS•	Roads, tracks, field and coastal paths
•LANDSCAPE•	Views to sea, with offshore rocks, rolling countryside
•SUGGESTED MAP•	aqua3 OS Explorer 316 Newcastle upon Tyne
•START / FINISH•	Grid reference: NZ 412635
•DOG FRIENDLINESS•	On leads on inland section of walk
•PARKING•	Whitburn Coastal Park car park, signed off A183 – turn right after entrance and drive to southern end of road
•PUBLIC TOILETS•	None on route
•CONTRIBUTOR•	David Winpenny

BACKGROUND TO THE WALK

The coast of Durham south of the Tyne was long renowned for its smugglers. The natural caves at the base of the cliffs of Marsden Bay provided hiding places for illicit activity. Most famous of the smugglers was Jack the Blaster, who in 1792 used explosives to increase the size of one of the caves, and provide steps from the cliff top. An entrepreneur, he sold refreshments to other smugglers. In the 19th century an underground ballroom was created here, and in the 1930s a lift was installed. It is now a popular pub and eating place called the Marsden Grotto.

The Punishment Hanging

One 18th-century smuggler turned informer to the customs men. His fellows discovered his treachery, and the smugglers' ship was prevented from landing its contraband cargo. As punishment the man was hanged in a basket in a shaft, now called Smugglers' Hole, near the Grotto, where he starved to death. On stormy nights his shrieks are said to be heard in the howling of the wind.

The Windmills of Cleadon

On the walk you will pass two windmills. The first, in Marsden, is a squat building that still retains its sails. The other, higher on Cleadon Hills, was built in the 1820s, and survived until the end of the century, when it was damaged in a storm. In World War Two it housed Royal Observer Corps members who scanned the North Sea for enemy aeroplanes. Looking south from the tower you will see the Greek temple that is the Penshaw Monument. A half-sized replica of the Temple of Theseus in Athens, it commemorates the 1st Earl of Durham, 'Radical Jack' Lambton, first Governor of Canada. As you cross the golf course beyond the windmill there are views north to Tynemouth, with its castle and priory on the headland north of the river.

The red-and-white striped Souter Lighthouse was opened in 1871 to protect ships from the notorious rocks called Whitburn Steel, just off the coast. It was the first light in the world to be electrically powered, by electric alternators. Originally it was nearly ¼ mile (400m) from the sea, but erosion has brought the cliff edge much nearer. Now decommissioned and in the care of the National Trust, the lighthouse and its surrounding buildings reward careful exploration. The grassy area north of the light, The Lees, was farmed until the 1930s, and then given to the local council as a park. The industrial buildings by the road are the remains of lime kilns, used by the local limestone quarries. South of the light, where Whitburn Coastal Park now lies, was from 1873 to 1968 the site of Whitburn Colliery.

Walk 26

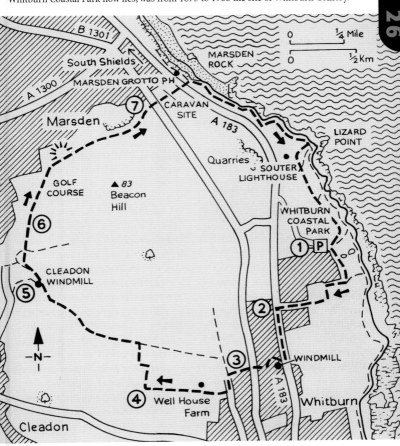

Walk 26 Directions

① Leave the car park at its southern end, following the gravel track toward the houses. The path winds and goes past a sign for **Whitburn Point Nature Reserve**. Follow the track ahead to go

through a gap in a wall and turn right. The path bends right, left and right again to join a road into houses. Go straight ahead to join the main road.

② Cross the road and turn left. Walk down the road until you reach the **windmill**. Turn right to enter

Walk 26

the grounds of the windmill. Go up the slope on the path and then between houses. Bear left then turn right to reach a T-junction.

③ Go straight ahead on a path that goes to the right of house **No 99**. When you reach another road turn left. Just after the first bungalow on the right, turn right along a signed track. Follow the track towards the farm. Go through the farmyard over two stiles and follow the lane beyond, with a hedge to your right. Where it ends, turn right over a stile.

> **WHILE YOU'RE THERE** ⓘ
> Visit **Arbeia Roman Fort** in South Shields. Built to supply the Roman army's campaign against the northern tribes, it has a full-size reconstruction of its gateway and a museum where you can see how Roman soldiers lived. You may even meet a member of the 'Cohors Quinta Gallorum' – volunteers dressed in Roman uniform.

④ Follow the path along the field edge. Go over another stile, gradually ascending. The path bends left then right, still following the field edge. Go over another two stiles. The path will bring you to the tower of **Cleadon Windmill**.

⑤ Go to the right of the windmill, following the wall on your right. Go right through a kissing gate, then bear slightly right (a brick tower to

> **WHERE TO EAT AND DRINK** ⓘ
> The **Marsden Grotto** near Marsden Rock has a restaurant, bar and bistro, catering for all tastes, from snacks to full meals (children welcome until 8:30PM, no dogs except guide dogs). Further south, **Souter Lighthouse** (children and guide dogs welcome) has a good National Trust tea room, with the chance to sit in the walled garden on sunny days – when the foghorn won't be working!

your left). Go parallel with the wall on your right. Cross a track and go through a wire mesh fence at right angles to the wall. Follow the path through scrubland to emerge by a yellow post by the **golf course**.

⑥ Cross the course, following the yellow posts and looking out for golfers. Go over a stone stile and turn right along a signed footpath, following the wall on your right. The path eventually descends beside houses to a road.

⑦ Cross and take the footpath almost opposite, to the right of a caravan site, heading towards the sea. Carefully cross the busy **A183** then turn right, following the sea edge. **Marsden Rock** is near by, and the **Marsden Grotto** to your left as you cross the road. Follow the coast as it bends left to **Lizard Point**. After a visit to **Souter Lighthouse**, continue ahead on a path slightly inland from the coast, which returns you to the car park.

> **WHAT TO LOOK FOR** ⓘ
> Off the coast at Marsden Bay are numerous **sea stacks** – pillars of rock that have been left as the sea has eroded the cliffs. The most famous of them is the largest, known as Marsden Rock. Although still impressive, it barely does justice to its fame. Until 1996 the rock was a naturally-formed arch; a second, smaller stack was joined to the rock on its south east side with a bridge of limestone. When this collapsed, the smaller stack had to be demolished as it was in a dangerous state. In the past there were ladders that gave access to the top for those willing to wade out, and local people used to have picnics there. There are even reports of choirs and brass bands giving impromptu concerts.

Romans and Countryfolk of Corbridge

Discover little Corbridge, where history lies around every corner.

•DISTANCE•	6 miles (9.7km)
•MINIMUM TIME•	3hrs 30min
•ASCENT / GRADIENT•	525ft (160m) ▲ ▲ ▲
•LEVEL OF DIFFICULTY•	🚶🚶 🚶🚶 🚶🚶
•PATHS•	Village streets, riverside and farm paths and lanes, 8 stiles
•LANDSCAPE•	Small town and low hills
•SUGGESTED MAP•	aqua3 OS Explorer OL43 Hadrian's Wall
•START / FINISH•	Grid reference: NY 992642
•DOG FRIENDLINESS•	Dogs should be on leads
•PARKING•	On town centre streets
•PUBLIC TOILETS•	On Princess Street between Hill Street and Main Street
•CONTRIBUTOR•	John Gillham

BACKGROUND TO THE WALK

Corbridge is a picturesque little town, with Georgian stone cottages, antique shops and old inns cuddled up to a square-towered church. Nothing much happens here these days: people come for a little peace and quiet away from the city and maybe a spot of Sunday lunch in one of those inns. The wide River Tyne flows by lazily on a journey that takes it from the wild hills of Northumberland, through the cityscapes of Newcastle and onwards to the shivering North Sea.

Roman Settlement

Though the present town was founded in Saxon times, the Romans, under Agricola, first arrived in AD 79. They established their settlement six years later, just ½ mile (800m) to the west of modern Corbridge, on the north bank of the Tyne. Known as Corstopitum, it would have been the most northerly settlement in the Roman Empire, strategically placed at the junction of their Dere Street (York to northern Britain) and Stanegate (Corbridge to Carlisle) roads, and near to what was, after AD 122, the frontier, Hadrian's Wall. The Romans also had a fine bridge across the Tyne, and you can still see the rubble remains of foundations when the water levels are low.

Defence against the Scots

In past centuries Corbridge was second only to Newcastle in this part of the world, and of great strategic importance. As such, the town has known many troubled times. You'll see that straight away, for the first house you come to, Low Hall on Main Street, has a fortified pele tower. These fortifications were added to defend against the Scots; both the marauding Border reivers, who came to rob and pillage, and the Scots armies, who came to destroy. William Wallace, Robert the Bruce and King David II all invaded and all laid the town waste on their journeys south. Centrepiece of modern Corbridge is undoubtedly St Andrews Church, built in the Saxon era and with a Roman archway borrowed from the older settlement. The church was extensively modified in the 13th century, with the addition of aisles, transepts and chancel, and was restored during Victorian times.

Round the back of the church you'll come across another fortified house, this time the 13th-century Vicar's Pele – even the clergy were not immune to the wrath of the Scots. Before going down to the River Tyne and that magnificent 17th-century bridge, the route passes Town Barns, where the famous north east based author Catherine Cookson lived in the 1970s.

We take a short riverside ramble now, before climbing out of the valley, traversing pastures scattered with woods, and strolling along hedge-lined country lanes. You arrive at Prospect Hill, with its pristine cottages and farmhouses. It does indeed have prospects – a fine view of Corbridge, the Tyne Valley and the low hills beyond where the Romans marched and Hadrian's Wall once offered a firm deterrent to those erring northerners.

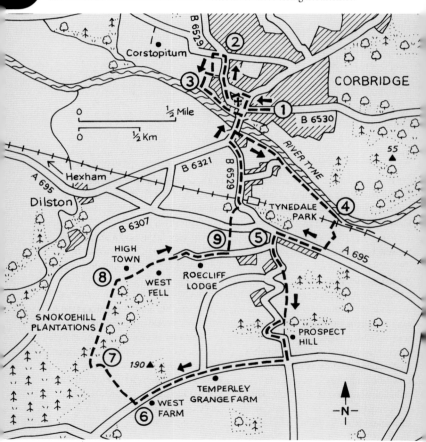

Walk 27 Directions

① The walk begins at **Low Hall Pele** on the eastern end of **Main Street**. Head west down Main Street

before turning right up **Princes Street**. At the town hall turn left along **Hill Street**, then, just before the church, turn left up the narrow street to pass the **Vicar's Pele**. Turn right at the **Market Place**

Walk 27

WHILE YOU'RE THERE
Visit the Roman Fort, **Corstopitum**, where the two large granaries and the Fountain House are particularly impressive. The main street that runs through is the Stanegate. Finds from the archaeological digs are kept in the museum. They include Roman armour, coins and other personal artefacts.

and head north up **Watling Street**, then **Stagshaw Road**, which is staggered to the left beyond the **Wheatsheaf Inn**.

② Go left along **Trinity Terrace** then left again along a footpath, signed 'West Green'. This leads past Catherine Cookson's old house, **Town Barns**, to the Georgian house of **Orchard Vale**, where you turn right, then left along a lane to the river.

③ Turn left along **Carelgate**, then follow the riverside path to the town bridge. Go over the bridge, then follow the south banks of the Tyne on an unsurfaced track that passes the cricket ground at **Tynedale Park** before mounting a grassy embankment running parallel to the river.

④ Turn right up some steps, go over a ladder stile, then cross the railway tracks (with care). Another stile and some more steps lead the path through a wood and across a field to meet the **A695** where you turn right – there's a footpath on the nearside.

⑤ Just beyond some cottages, turn left up a country lane, which zig-zags up **Prospect Hill**. Just after the first bend leave the lane for a southbound path that climbs fields. Just short of some woods the path meets a track where you turn right

for a few paces to rejoin the lane. Follow this up to reach a crossroads at the top of the hill, where you turn right.

⑥ After passing **Temperley Grange** and **West farms** leave the road for a path on the right that follows first the right-hand side, then the left-hand side of a dry-stone wall across high fields and down to the **Snokoehill Plantations**.

WHERE TO EAT AND DRINK
The **Angel** on Main Street is a large 17th-century coaching inn that offers a fine range of tasty meals, including Sunday roasts. It's a free house with Black Sheep and Courage ales always available. Children are welcome.

⑦ Go through a gate to enter the wood, then turn left along a track running along the top edge. The track doubles back to the right, soon to follow the bottom edge of the woods.

⑧ Turn right beyond a gate above **High Town farm** and follow the track, which becomes tarred beyond **West Fell**.

⑨ Beyond **Roecliff Lodge** a path on the left crosses a field to reach the **A695** road. Across the other side of the road the path continues and enters a copse known as **The Scrogs**, before joining the **B6529** by **Corbridge Railway Station**. Follow this over the bridge and back into **Corbridge** itself.

WHAT TO LOOK FOR
In an old stableyard wall behind the Wheatsheaf Inn (off Watling Street) there are two crudely **sculpted heads** believed to have come from one of the three Corbridge churches set ablaze by the invading Scots in the early 14th century.

Historic Hexham

A walk round and about the abbey and market town of Hexham.

•DISTANCE•	3¾ miles (6km)
•MINIMUM TIME•	2hrs
•ASCENT / GRADIENT•	590ft (180m) ▲ ▲ ▲
•LEVEL OF DIFFICULTY•	🚶🚶 🚶🚶 🚶🚶
•PATHS•	Town streets, lanes and woodland paths, 4 stiles
•LANDSCAPE•	Market town and small wooded valleys
•SUGGESTED MAP•	aqua3 OS Explorer OL43 Hadrian's Wall
•START / FINISH•	Grid reference: NY 939641
•DOG FRIENDLINESS•	Can run free in woods of Cowgarth Dene and Wydon Burn
•PARKING•	Pay-and-display car park, next to supermarket
•PUBLIC TOILETS•	At car park, by tourist information centre
•CONTRIBUTOR•	John Gillham

BACKGROUND TO THE WALK

It was AD 674 and the Romans had been gone over 200 years. Their wall lay crumbling on the green hills to the north, high above the valley of the Tyne. These were the early days of Christianity, and the first monasteries and abbeys were being established. Queen Etheldra of Northumbria had given Bishop Wilfred the land by the river and here, at Hexham, he would build his priory.

Wlifred's Priory

Wilfred had travelled far and wide, including to Rome, and had been impressed by the splendour and majesty of many European churches. His would be a magnificent one with 'crypts of beautifully finished stone… walls of wonderful height and length'. Many of the stones in his great building were Roman, removed from the fort at Corbridge. The monastery became a cathedral and a renowned centre of learning. However, these were dark days and places like this were rich pickings for Viking raiders. The priory was to be attacked on many occasions, but in AD 875 Halfdene the Dane, who had ransacked much of the county, finally burned it down. Although attempts were made, it wasn't until 1113, when the Augustinians were awarded the land and started the present abbey, that it was restored to its former majesty.

The abbey buildings survived Henry VIII's dissolution of the monasteries of the 1530s because they were was also used as a parish church. Instead of being demolished, Hexham was embellished and extended. The original crypt was retained intact too, and is now surely one of the finest Saxon structures to be found anywhere in Britain. While the nave and transepts date back to the 12th and 13th centuries, Dobson's East End and Temple Moore's nave were constructed between 1850 and 1910.

The Riot Act

In the shadow of the abbey, and also constructed with the help of Roman masonry, are the 14th-century Moot Hall and also the Manor Office, which was the first purpose-built gaol in Britain. The two buildings will be the first points of interest you'll see on the walk. Through the arch of the Moot Hall you come to the Market Square, which in 1761 became the scene of a major tragedy. Angry lead miners from Allendale, who were objecting to their conscription to the local militia, descended on Hexham in protest. On this spot they were read the Riot Act. Fighting broke out and, by the end of the day, over 300 miners were injured and 50 had been killed. The North Yorkshire Militia, who were responsible for the atrocity, were subsequently known as the Hexham Butchers.

View of the Town

Past Benson's Monument the walk comes to the edge of the old part of town and side-steps most of the new by climbing the southern hillsides along a wooded dell, known as Cowgarth Dene. The little stream here provided water for the monks of the priory. At the ominously named Black House you're at the top of the walk and can see Hexham and the valley that Wilfred inherited.

Walk 28

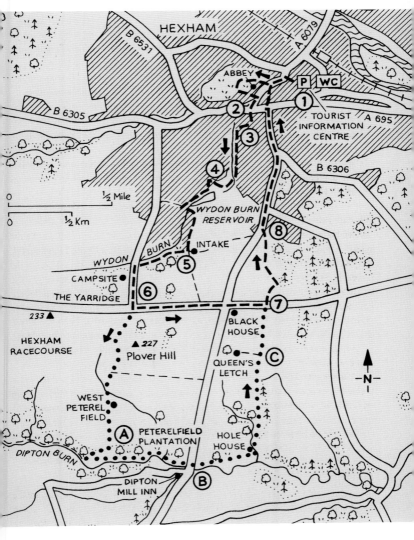

Walk 28 Directions

① From the car park (not the supermarket end) take the exit between the tourist information centre and the café to follow a narrow street past the **Old Gaol**. Go under the arches of the **Moot Hall** and enter the **Market Place**. Take a tour of **The Sele**, the park grounds surrounding Hexham Abbey, before aiming roughly south west across them to the Queen Hall on **Beaumont Street**.

WHILE YOU'RE THERE ⓘ

Great Chesters, known to the Romans as Cilurnum and set on the banks of the North Tyne near Chollerford, is a wonderfully preserved cavalry fort with a fine museum founded by keen archaeologist John Clayton (▶ Walk 31).

---

② Turn right along here to reach **Benson's Monument** then continue straight ahead on an unnamed street. After taking the first turning on the right ignore Elvaston Road on the left, but instead go straight ahead on a tarred lane that leads to the foot of the wooded **Cowgarth Dene**.

③ When you get to a bridge, turn off into the woodland where the now unsurfaced track crosses a footbridge and climbs out to a little park at the edge of a modern housing estate. Follow the woodland edge, then a track past a water treatment works.

WHERE TO EAT AND DRINK ⓘ

At the **County Hotel** on Priestpopple in the heart of Hexham you can enjoy morning coffee or dine well at their Cromwell Restaurant where they use prime produce, sourced wherever possible from local farms.

---

④ On nearing a housing estate, go through a gate on the left then double-back left on a path by some houses. Where the path turns right, climb some steps on to a track that runs along the north side of **Wydon Burn Reservoir**, now filled with reeds and tall grasses, not water.

⑤ Turn left along the lane then, at **Intake farm**, turn right along a path that leads into the thick woodland of Wydon Burn's upper reaches. A narrow path continues through the woods to reach the lane at **Causey Hill** where you turn left past the campsite to a junction with a road known as The Yarridge. The modern building you'll see here is part of the **Hexham Racecourse**.

⑥ Turn left along the road and go straight ahead at the crossroads.

⑦ Beyond **Black House** a stile on the left marks the start of a downhill, cross-field path into Hexham. Beyond a step stile the path veers right to round some gorse bushes before resuming its course alongside the left field edge.

⑧ Just before reaching a whitewashed cottage go over the stile on the left and follow the road down into the town. Turn left along the shopping street at the bottom, then right along **St Mary's Chare**, back to the **Market Place**.

WHAT TO LOOK FOR ⓘ

St Wilfrid's Seat, a 1,300-year-old frith (sanctuary) stool from the original priory was sculpted from a block of stone and survived the Danish attacks. Some believe it to have been the coronation throne of the early Northumbrian kings, though it may well have been a bishops' throne. You'll find it in the middle of the choir in Hexham Abbey.

And on to Hexhamshire

Through the countryside where a queen fled from her mortal enemies.
See map and information panel for Walk 28

•DISTANCE•	5½ miles (8.8km)
•MINIMUM TIME•	3hrs 30min
•ASCENT / GRADIENT•	984ft (300m)
•LEVEL OF DIFFICULTY•	

Walk 29 Directions (Walk 28 option)

This route goes a bit further, to the fringe of Hexhamshire Common, a low-lying area of heather moor that stretches out to the western edge of Northumberland.

Leave Walk 28 at Point ⑥, the road known as **The Yarridge**. Across the road go over a ladder stile and follow a path across the first of many fields. The Hexham (National Hunt) Racecourse circuit and its buildings lie to the right. Through a gateway, cut diagonally left across the second field to a step stile in the boundary fence. The path heads south across two more fields, then follows an unsurfaced lane to the farm at **West Peterel Field**. Now you can see the Hexhamshire hills, which rise from the long, narrow wooded dene of **Dipton Burn**.

Beyond the farm the path follows a fence on the right as it descends towards the dene. After crossing a stile in the last field, the path changes to the other side of the fence, before raking down into the woods. At the far end of a clearing double back along a clear track which soon re-enters the woodland of the **Peterelfield Plantation** (Point Ⓐ). There are many paths through the woods – stay with the main one that never strays too far from the burn. It emerges at the roadside close to ivy-clad **Dipton Mill Inn** (Point Ⓑ) – an ideal stop for lunch. Across the road follow a track past an old mill building before continuing along a burnside path. At the paddocks, ignore the gate on the left but follow the perimeter path over the stile on the right – a recent diversion. Opposite **Hole House** turn left, following the path to the right of the cottage. Bear left over a footbridge, then climb through woodland.

At the top gate the route climbs across fields at the woodland edge then continues north past **Queen's Letch** (Point Ⓒ), a derelict farm. The Battle of Hexham Levels had ended in defeat for the Lancastrians. Queen Margaret of Anjou was fleeing with Edward, Prince of Wales, when her horse slipped on these slopes (a letch meant a slip in those times). They were befriended by a robber, who guided them to the Queen's Cave, 2 miles (3.2km) upstream.

Meet the road at Point ⑦, east of **Black House farm** and follow Walk 28 back to **Hexham**.

Castle Eden's Gorge

A walk through an important National Nature Reserve displaying impressive woodland and geological scenery.

Walk 30

•DISTANCE•	4½ miles (7.2km)
•MINIMUM TIME•	2hrs 30min
•ASCENT / GRADIENT•	295ft (90m)
•LEVEL OF DIFFICULTY•	
•PATHS•	Mostly good but sometimes steep and muddy
•LANDSCAPE•	Heavily wooded river gorge
•SUGGESTED MAP•	aqua3 OS Explorer 308 Durham & Sunderland
•START / FINISH•	Grid reference: NZ 427393
•DOG FRIENDLINESS•	Can be off lead
•PARKING•	Car park at Oakerside Dene Lodge
•PUBLIC TOILETS•	None on route
•CONTRIBUTOR•	Anthony Toole

Walk 30 Directions

Castle Eden Dene is the longest river gorge on the Durham coast. It takes its name from the estate and village that lie south. The Burdon family bought the estate in 1758 and by 1780, had built the castle to a design by Newcastle architect, William Newton. The dene was incorporated into the estate in 1790 and its many pathways were created for the enjoyment of the Burdons – one such path, still known as Miss Mary's Walk, was a favourite of a daughter of the family.

After the death of Rowland Burdon, the last of the family, the dene was taken over by Peterlee Development Corporation in 1951. Its recreational and leisure potential was one factor taken into account when Peterlee was chosen as the site for a new town in the late 1940s. In 1985, English Nature declared Castle Eden Dene a National Nature Reserve and later, in view of the quality of the wildlife experience it offers, classified it as one of 31 Spotlight reserves in England.

The bedrock of the gorge consists of magnesian limestone, laid down by seas that covered the area 250 million years ago. This was later covered by boulder clay from the glaciers of the last ice age. Castle Eden Burn has cut through these layers to form the gorge, which, at Gunner's Pool, is only a few yards wide. Elsewhere, steep slopes end abruptly in limestone crags, while collapse of the walls has strewn the valley floor with large boulders.

The whole dene is heavily wooded with oak, ash, beech, lime and various conifers. As the largest yew

WHILE YOU'RE THERE

A more spectacular exposition of the **magnesian limestone geology** can be seen on the cliffs at Blackhall, just south of the mouth of Castle Eden Dene. Here, the sea has eroded the rocks to form cliffs, caves, arches and stacks.

forest in the north of England it has been designated a Special Area of Conservation under the European Habitats Directive. Fallen trees are left to decay and become homes for fungi and invertebrates. Plants include over 100 species of moss, nearly 30 liverworts and more than 300 flowers. Animals that dwell here include foxes, roe deer, badgers and both red and grey squirrels. The flowers attract butterflies, notably the Eden argus, a rare variant of the northern brown argus.

WHAT TO LOOK FOR   ⓘ

It is estimated that there are over 30 **roe deer** in the dene, although they usually remain well hidden. **Grey squirrels** are easily seen. In conifer areas, where deciduous trees are kept under control by English Nature staff, **red squirrels** are able to hold their own against the greys.

From the car park, go through a kissing gate and follow the track downhill. At a junction marked by a wooden post with a picture of a squirrel, take the right track back uphill. Continue on this main track, ignoring the next squirrel marker post, to reach the boundary fence of the **Peterlee** housing estate. Keeping the fence to your right, follow a track almost as far as the **A19** road. Turn left and go steeply down through woods to a tunnel leading under the road.

Turn left through a kissing gate, then down steps to a bridge on the right. Cross and continue up more steps to a junction with a track at the edge of a golf course. Follow this to the left. Where it forks, by a gate into the golf course, take the right fork. The track leads downhill, crossing a small bridge, and later two larger bridges over a loop in the river. Go steadily uphill, swinging

left at the top. The undulating track leads, after a few hundred yards, to **Gunner's Pool Bridge**.

Visit the bridge to see the narrowest and most spectacular part of the gorge. Return to the track and follow it uphill across another bridge. The track zig-zags more steeply to reach the edge of the golf course again and a view of Castle Eden. The track continues downhill. When it forks, take the right fork and follow this to another fork. This time, go left. You are now on **Miss Mary's Walk**.

When the track again splits, follow the left branch through thick yew forest, then along the edge of cultivated fields and around the head of a subsidiary valley. At a stile by an English Nature notice board, go downhill, then left at the next fork. This brings you to the main road on the valley floor. To your right is **Garden of Eden Bridge**.

Follow the road to the left, along the river bank, past two touching boulders called the **Kissing Frogs** and a tree-covered boulder, the **Devil's Lapstone**. Cross the river via the second bridge, **Dungy Bridge**, and pass a huge boulder supported by concrete pillars. Pass crags on both banks of the river, the most spectacular being **White Rock**. At the next fork, go right, uphill to a junction. Turn right again to return to the car park.

WHERE TO EAT AND DRINK   ⓘ

About ¼ mile (400m) from Oakerside Dene Lodge is the **Oaklands** public house, a modern building, in keeping with the surrounding housing estate. Food is served each day in a conservatory. There is also a family dining area with a children's playzone.

Walk 31

Along the Emperor's Wall

See life from the perspective of both Roman soldier and Scots warrior.

•DISTANCE•	8 miles (12.9km)
•MINIMUM TIME•	4hrs
•ASCENT / GRADIENT•	885ft (270m) ▲ ▲ ▲
•LEVEL OF DIFFICULTY•	👫 👫 👫
•PATHS•	Mainly well walked National Trails, 16 stiles
•LANDSCAPE•	Ridge and wild moorland
•SUGGESTED MAP•	aqua3 OS Explorer OL43 Hadrian's Wall
•START / FINISH•	Grid reference: NY 750677
•DOG FRIENDLINESS•	Farming country, keep dogs on lead
•PARKING•	Steel Rigg (pay) car park
•PUBLIC TOILETS•	Nearest at Housesteads information centre
•NOTE•	Please don't damage wall by walking on it
•CONTRIBUTOR•	John Gillham

BACKGROUND TO THE WALK

After a visit in AD 122, Roman Emperor Hadrian decided that his Governor of Britain, Nepos, would supervise the building of a great wall to repel the violent Picts and Britons of the north. They originally planned it to span the countryside between the River Irthing at Thirlwall and Newcastle, but added a turf wall that would extend to the west coast at Bowness on Solway.

Impressive Feat of Engineering

The engineers were put to work, aided by Roman soldiers from York, Caerleon and Chester. The first-built sections of the castellated wall were 15ft (4.5m) high and 10ft (3m) wide though later sections were reduced in size in order to speed up the construction. On the northern side the Romans excavated a V-shaped ditch, the Berm, 27ft (8.2m) wide and 9ft (2.7m) deep, except where defending crags made this unnecessary. Fortified gateways, milecastles, were sited along the length of the wall at 1 Roman mile (1.5km) intervals. They would allow passage for through traffic, and also act as a barracks for eight soldiers. Between the milecastles, at intervals of ⅓ Roman mile (498m), were turrets, which served as observation posts. Later large forts like Great Chesters, Carvoran and Housesteads were built close to the wall, and a second ditch, the Vallum, was dug on the south side to enclose the military area. This was a flat-bottomed trench 20ft (6m) wide and 10ft (3m) deep.

After the Roman withdrawal from Britain the wall fell into decay and its crumbling masonry was used to build churches, farmhouses and field walls. After Bonnie Prince Charlie's 1745 rebellion the parliament demanded that a military road be built. Unfortunately it used Hadrian's Wall as its foundations for many miles. It seemed that the wall would disintegrate into oblivion. The fact that modern-day visitors can still view this spectacle is largely due to the efforts of entrepreneur and keen archaeologist, John Clayton (1792–1890). He bought much of the land that contained the wall, and presided over the early digs that unearthed its treasures. The foundations of the wall and its forts have since been lovingly restored. The museum at Chesters remains a testament to this great man.

As you stride out beside Hadrian's Wall and above the precipitous cliffs, it is not difficult to imagine the desolate times of the Roman cohorts patrolling along the high parapets. Looking to the north you can see the dark, brooding moors where the northern tribes people lay watching. And when it is time to explore those dark moors, take the time to look back to the wall, to those whin sill cliffs silhouetted against the sky, and appreciate what a great deterrent this must have been.

Walk 31 Directions

① From the car park descend to a grassy depression beneath **Peel Crags**. The path arcs left and climbs back to the ridge in a series of steps before following the cliff tops past **Turret 39a** and **Milecastle 39**.

② There's another dip, then a climb to **Highshield Crags**, which

Walk 31

overlook Crag Lough. Beyond the lake the footpath climbs past **Hotbank farm**

③ At the next dip, **Rapishaw Gap**, turn left over the ladder stile and follow the faint but waymarked **Pennine Way** route across undulating moorland. The first stile lies in the far right corner of a large rushy enclosure. A clear cart track develops beyond a dyke and climbs to a ridge on **Ridley Common** where you turn half left to descend a grassy ramp.

④ The path slowly arcs right to meet and cross a fenced cart track at **Cragend**. Here a clear grass track zig-zags down to a moorland depression with **Greenlee Lough** in full view to your left. At the bottom the ground can be marshy and the path becomes indistinct in places. A waymark points a sharp right turn but the path loses itself on the bank above it. Head north here, keeping the farmhouse of **East Stonefolds** at ten to the hour. The next stile lies in a kink in the cross wall.

⑤ Beyond this, turn half left to traverse a field before going over a ladder stile and turning left along the farm track which passes through East Stonefolds. The track ends at **West Stonefolds**. The right of way is supposed to go through the farm and over a stile on the

right past the farmhouse. However, they encourage you to take the direct alternative route in a field at the back of the farm (on the right) by leaving a 'dogs running free' sign and an alsation in the yard.

⑥ Past the house continue, with a wall to the left, along a grassy ride, and go over a step stile to reach a signposted junction of routes. Go straight ahead on the permissive path signposted to the Greenlee Lough Birdhide. The path follows a fence down to the lake. Ignore the stile unless you want to go to the hide itself, but instead continue alongside the fence.

⑦ Go over the next stile and cross wetlands north of the lake on a duckboard path, which soon swings right to a gate. Beyond this continue on the path, climbing north west, guided by waymarker posts to the farm track by the conifers of the **Greenlee Plantation**.

⑧ Turn left along the track and follow it past **Gibbs Hill farm**. Past the farmhouse a tarmac lane leads back towards the wall. Turn left at the T-junction to return to the car park.

The Gorgeous Grounds of Allen Banks

Walking through a wooded gorge to Dickie's watchtower.

•DISTANCE•	5 miles (8km)
•MINIMUM TIME•	2hrs 45min
•ASCENT / GRADIENT•	420ft (128m)
•LEVEL OF DIFFICULTY•	
•PATHS•	Well-signposted woodland paths, 7 stiles
•LANDSCAPE•	Wooded river valley
•SUGGESTED MAP•	aqua3 OS Explorer OL43 Hadrian's Wall
•START / FINISH•	Grid reference: NY 798640
•DOG FRIENDLINESS•	Dogs should be under close control
•PARKING•	Car park included in fee for walk (► Note below)
•PUBLIC TOILETS•	At car park
•NOTE•	Early part of walk is not right of way, National Trust makes small charge per adult to walk here
•CONTRIBUTOR•	John Gillham

BACKGROUND TO THE WALK

After having an easy youth in the high Northumbrian moors and dales, the East and West Allen rivers join forces at Cupola. There's only 4 miles (6.4km) to go as the crow flies to get to the wide lazy waters of the South Tyne, but the Allen will be put through its paces as the hills in the east and west close in. Even in the last stretch the river has to wriggle and squeeze through a tight gorge between Ridley Common and Morralee Fell. This last place is known as Allen Banks and has, for centuries, been cloaked with thick woodland – a spot of great beauty.

Designing the Grounds

Allen Banks was part of the Ridley Hall Estate, whose history goes back to medieval times when the Ridley family presided here. The original hall was destroyed by a great fire in the middle of the 18th century and the magnificent sandstone mansion you see today is Georgian. John Davidson of Otterburn purchased the estate in the 1830s for his wife Susan, granddaughter of the 9th Earl of Strathmore. In those times the valley was mined for both coal and lead. Susan Davidson took a keen interest in the grounds and not only laid out the formal gardens, but designed a network of paths through the wilder environs of the riverside and woods. The Davidsons were childless, and on their deaths the estate passed to John Bowes and his French wife, Josephine (► While You're There, Walk 47). It was the Bowes-Lyon family who gave Allen Banks to the National Trust in 1942.

Nature Reserve

Beyond the car park, which is sited on the hall's old kitchen garden, the hills close in, with Raven Crag towering above to the right and Morralee Fell on the far banks to the left. The river bends to the right and soon you enter the nature reserve at Briarwood Banks. After Plankey Mill the route climbs out of the valley and comes across the crumbling remains of

Staward Pele. This 14th-century fortified house was once owned by the Dukes of York and leased to the monks of Hexham. Later it fell into the hands of Dickie of Kingswood, a local character and petty criminal. Although today the old house is tangled with scrub, in better times it would have had a commanding view of the valley and any invading border reivers. In Dickie's case, the police wouldn't have been confident about carrying out a successful raid if he had been suspected of any wrongdoing.

Walk 32 Directions

① Follow the riverside path from the back of the car park and stay with the lower left fork where the path divides. Stay on the Allen's west banks rather than crossing the suspension bridge. Beyond it the path tucks beneath **Raven Crag**. The river bends to the right and you soon enter the nature reserve at

> **WHILE YOU'RE THERE** ⓘ
> **Vindolanda** and the **Roman Army Museum** north of Haltwistle are a must for those who want to discover all things Roman. Agricola first established Vindolanda around AD 85 as a turf fort to guard the Roman road known as the Stanegate. There's a reconstruction of the old turf wall and a timber milecastle. The museum has a superb collection of Roman armour, boots and shoes, jewellery and coins. The archaeological digs are still going on and new finds are added regularly.

Briarwod Banks. Here the ancient woodland has seen continuous growth dating back to the end of the last ice age, some 10,000 years ago. With broadleaved trees like sessile oak, wych elm, ash, birch, rowan and alder flourishing this is a haven for wildlife, and over 60 species of bird have been recorded in the valley. These include the sparrowhawk, tawny owl, wood warbler, woodcock and song thrush.

② On Briarwood Banks the path uses a footbridge across **Kingswood Burn**, then turns left to cross the suspension bridge across the **Allen**. You are now at **Plankey Mill**.

> **WHERE TO EAT AND DRINK** ⓘ
> The **Bowes Hotel**, Bardon Mil, has recently been refurbished and has a smart restaurant with a blackboard full of specials. Children are welcome and there's wheelchair access. Not open for meals Sunday evenings and Mondays.

③ Turn right along the field-edge path close to the river and go over either of two step stiles back into woodland. If you chose the riverside stile some steps will lead you back to the main track. You are now

following the green waymarks of the **Staward Pele path** which stays close to the river, though it's often high above the banks. Just beyond a footbridge the path divides. Take the right fork – the left is your downhill return route.

④ On reaching the top eastern edge of the woods the path turns left where it first passes the gatehouse of **Staward Pele** then the ruins of the fortified farm itself.

⑤ Beyond the pele the track descends, steeply, sometimes in steps back to the previously mentioned footbridge. Retrace your steps to **Plankey Mill**.

⑥ On reaching the tarred lane by the mill, turn right, go uphill along it, then, at a sharp bend, turn off it on to an enclosed footpath. This leads to a another footpath that follows a field edge alongside the river's east bank.

⑦ Turn left over the suspension bridge opposite the **Morralee Wood** turn off, then turn right along the outward footpath back to the car park.

> **WHAT TO LOOK FOR** ⓘ
> **Mink** have been regularly seen in the valley. This brown, weasel-like mammal is about 12–20in (30–51cm) in length with short legs and a long neck. The species was originally imported from the forests of the United States and intended to be farmed for its prized pelts. Many have since escaped or been released into the wild where they have become a very successful predator to fish and also birds as large as geese and ducks. The mink generally hunts in the dim light of daybreak or in the evening, but in the dismal days of winter they are frequently visible during daylight hours.

Valley of the Shining Water

Exploring one of Northumberland's most attractive river valleys.

Walk 33

•DISTANCE•	3¾ miles (6km)
•MINIMUM TIME•	2hrs 15min
•ASCENT / GRADIENT•	590ft (180m) ▲ ▲ ▲
•LEVEL OF DIFFICULTY•	🚶 🚶 🚶
•PATHS•	Good river paths and faint field paths, 19 stiles
•LANDSCAPE•	Riverside and high pasture
•SUGGESTED MAP•	aqua3 OS Explorer OL43 Hadrian's Wall
•START / FINISH•	Grid reference: NY 838558
•DOG FRIENDLINESS•	Farming country, keep dogs on leads
•PARKING•	Ample parking in village centre
•PUBLIC TOILETS•	In village centre
•CONTRIBUTOR•	John Gillham

BACKGROUND TO THE WALK

If you were dropped into East Allendale you could be forgiven for thinking you were in the northern part of the Yorkshire Dales. Like that area it's rugged rather than beautiful, but it's also peaceful and serene. Appropriately, Allen comes from the Celtic word 'aln' which means shining or foaming. The main centre, Allendale Town, is set on a hillside overlooking a bend in the East Allen River and sheltered beneath the heather moors of Hexhamshire Common. It proclaims itself to be the true geographical centre of Britain, and co-ordinates inscribed on to the church tower's sundial reinforce this.

Mining Town

On entering the large Market Square with its many large hotels and inns, it soon becomes obvious that this place has seen busier times, and so it has. This was a mining town, the most prosperous in the whole of the region, with good veins of lead and silver. In the halcyon days of the 18th century Allendale had a population of over 5,500, four times what it is today. Allendale was lively, for the miners were hard-working, hard-drinking men who filled each and everyone of the inns. Even with the death of their industry at the turn of the century, the place stayed busy, with motor coaches bringing people from the industrial north east for health and enjoyment.

Perhaps Allendale is most famous for its Baal Fire Festival, which takes place each New Year's Eve. It's said to be of Viking origin. At 11:30PM the pubs empty and a crowd gathers in the square. Suddenly the night sky is lit up by a procession of 40 men dressed in fancy costumes and with flaming tar barrels on their heads. The men, known as guisers, parade around the town streets accompanied by the Allendale Silver Band. Close to midnight the guisers hurl the burning contents of the barrels on to a bonfire, whose flames then explode high into the sky. It's a dangerous procedure, usually resulting in a few singed eyebrows. The church bells chime in the New Year and everybody sings *Auld Lang Syne* before returning to the pub for more celebrations.

There are many long walks from Allendale Town to the moors but a good introduction explores the immediate environs of the valley itself. Passing the old inns you go down to the

Walk 33

river, which is lined by fine stands of trees. In spring and early summer the fields and woods will be full of wild flowers like bloody cranesbill, wild primrose, herb Robert and ragwort.

Later the walk climbs away, to high fields and old farms looking down on the rooftops of Allendale Town. The river, in some places hidden by trees, but in others shining among the valley meadows, meanders into the distance to those dark North Pennine moors that yawn across the western skies.

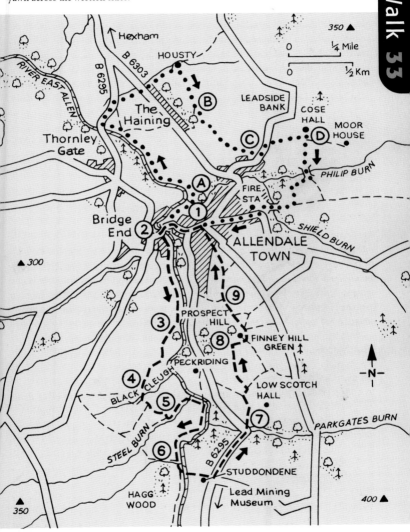

Walk 33 Directions

① From the **Market Place** take the Whitfield road down past the **Hare and Hounds** and round the left-

hand bend to the old **Mill Bridge** across the **River East Allen**.

② Immediately beyond the bridge, turn left along a tarred lane past some cottages – it's highlighted by a

Walk 33

footpath sign 'to Wooley Scar'. Where the track swings right leave it and go through the gate ahead before following a cross-field path, parallel to the river.

③ At the narrow end of a wedge shaped field go over a ladder stile on the right. Here the path veers away from the river and enters an area above **Wooley Scar**, which can be slightly overgrown with nettles and ragwort in the summer months. The route continues generally south west across fields.

> **WHERE TO EAT AND DRINK**
> The **Kings Head**, in the square, is one of many fine inns and a favourite of mine. There's a huge blackboard with a wide variety of meals on offer in the bar, with a real log fire. Children are welcome and dogs are allowed in the bar.

④ Beyond **Black Cleugh** it swings south east along a short section of rutted track. Ignoring the first stile on the right follow the right field edge. A waymark on a broken fence points the way down towards the woods surrounding **Steel Burn**.

⑤ Turn left along a grass track running parallel to the burn and go through a gate behind a little cottage. Turn right over a footbridge crossing the burn, then follow the banks of the **East Allen**.

> **WHILE YOU'RE THERE**
> Killhope Wheel is the pride of the **North of England Lead Mining Museum** at the head of Weardale. Around 33ft (10m) in diameter the wrought iron water wheel towers above the crushing mill site. They'll give you a hard hat and lamp before leading you underground to the mine face. It's open every day from late March to the end of September and on October weekends.

> **WHAT TO LOOK FOR**
> On Dryburn Moor, west of the River East Allen, you'll notice some old **chimneys**. They're connected to the flues from the Allenmill Smelt Mill. The two brick-built flues drew off the sulphurous fumes and created a draught to stoke the smelting furnaces. The draught also caused the silver content of the fumes to condense on the walls where it could be recovered.

The clear route crosses riverside meadows and ignores the first river footbridge near **Peckriding**.

⑥ After meandering with the river, the path comes upon a track near **Hagg Wood** and follows it across a bridge over the East Allen. The track zig-zags past the farm at **Studdondene** to reach the **B6295** where you turn left.

⑦ On reaching the woods of **Parkgates Burn** take the left of two waymarked paths. Over a stile it climbs fields towards the left of two farmhouses on the skyline – **Low Scotch Hall**. It turns right then left to round the farmhouse, now following the left field edge high above the valley.

⑧ On reaching the woods of **Prospect Hill** turn right through some animal pens then along an enclosed path to the farm of **Finney Hill Green**. Turn left beyond the house and continue along the left edge of three fields.

⑨ A modern housing estate at the edge of **Allendale Town** comes into view and the path heads north, parallel to the houses. In the last field it descends towards some more mature housing and enters an estate through a little ginnel. Go past the children's playground and out on to the main road in the village centre.

To the Edge of the Moor

By river bank, meadow and woods to the fringes of Hexhamshire.
See map and information panel for Walk 33

•DISTANCE•	3 miles (4.8km)
•MINIMUM TIME•	1hr 45min
•ASCENT / GRADIENT•	525ft (160m)
•LEVEL OF DIFFICULTY•	

Walk 34 Directions
(Walk 33 option)

From the centre of Allendale Town (Point ①), take the Whitfield road and turn right before the **Mill Bridge** on an enclosed path, signposted to Allen Mill. The path descends to the banks of the **River East Allen** and follows it north through its tree-filled valley.

Here you see a barred up entrance to the **Blackett Level** (Point Ⓐ). This is part of a curtailed scheme to drain the valley's lead mines and provide waterpower to turn the machinery. It was originally intended to drill the shaft all the way to Allenheads (7 miles/11.3km) but after 40 years and a good few problems the scheme was halted well short at Sipton.

At the road at **Allen Mill** turn right before taking the second of two cross-field footpaths. This leads towards the houses of **The Haining**, which line the Catton road. The footpath by the side of the last house is not waymarked but climbs towards the farmhouse of **Housty**. If the path is too steep for you, a zig-zag grass track will lead you to the top field below the farmhouse.

Turn right through a gateway, go over a ladder stile, then follow the field edge, on the right. On reaching a wood (Point Ⓑ) turn right through a gate, then left to go through a series of gates and to follow an overgrown path alongside the wood's western perimeter. The trackless path now traces the top edge of two fields before crossing a ladder stile and turning right. The route now follows a narrow path down to a lane known as **Leadside Bank** (Point Ⓒ).

Turn left and climb the lane before turning right along a farm track signposted to Moor House. Leave the track just short of **Cose Hall** (Point Ⓓ) and head for the stile to the right of the farmhouse. Once over, turn right to the bottom left edge of the field, then follow the wall on the left in the next field before crossing **Philip Burn** on a footbridge. Climb the far banks, go over another stile, then turn right along a fence. The path turns left at the field corner and passes through a small wood. At an intersection of paths go over the stile and turn right. Steps lead down to the footbridge over **Shield Burn** and more climb up to the lane at the other side. Turn left along the lane then right, passing the fire station to return to the village centre.

Perfect Blanchland

Honey-coloured buildings and a wooded valley make Blanchland a picture-book village.

Walk 35

•DISTANCE•	3½ miles (5.7km)
•MINIMUM TIME•	1hr 30min
•ASCENT / GRADIENT•	345ft (105m) ▲ ▲ ▲
•LEVEL OF DIFFICULTY•	🚶 🚶 🚶
•PATHS•	Tracks and field paths, two short climbs
•LANDSCAPE•	Village and wooded farmland
•SUGGESTED MAP•	aqua3 OS Explorer 307 Consett & Derwent Reservoir
•START / FINISH•	Grid reference: NY 964504
•DOG FRIENDLINESS•	On lead, except final riverside path from Blanchland Bridge
•PARKING•	Blanchland car park, at north edge of village
•PUBLIC TOILETS•	Blanchland, near bridge
•CONTRIBUTOR•	David Winpenny

Walk 35 Directions

From the car park turn left up the road. This was once a drove road, used to bring cattle from Hexham over Blanchland Moor. Higher up the road are the remains of lead mines and a ruined engine house – a reminder that Blanchland was home to several generations of miners in the 18th and early 19th centuries. Go left up the walled track towards **Coat House**.

As the track bends right towards a farmhouse, go left through a waymarked gate and cross the small

---

WHILE YOU'RE THERE ⓘ

Derwent Reservoir, east of Blanchland, is second in size only to Kielder Water in the north. It has a surface area of 1,000 acres (405ha), and was completed in 1967. The activities it offers include sailing and windsurfing, as well as fishing. The Northumberland and Durham county boundary goes through the middle of the lake, following the old river course.

---

field to go over a ladder stile. Bear half left down the hillside on a faint track to a ladder stile on to the road. Turn right into the hamlet of **Baybridge**. As you approach the stone bridge you enter County Durham – the boundary leaves the River Derwent at this point to take in Durham County Council's Baybridge picnic site.

Cross the bridge over the river. Opposite the road to the right, go left on a signed footpath by a gate. Just after crossing a stream, go right, uphill, by a waymarked post. Climb the hill to a waymarked stile. Cross the field beyond then bear right to follow the fence. At the top, go left through a gateway and follow the track, which bears right round a wall. Go through two gates into the farmyard at **Allenshields**.

Go straight ahead though another gate and ahead across the field to a ladder stile. Follow the field edge, over another ladder stile, then bear half left to leave the field by a gate

Walk 35

near the house. Turn left down the lane. Turn left at the T-junction and cross the bridge into **Blanchland**. The view of Blanchland, as you descend to the 18th-century bridge, is of a pretty stone-built village that clusters around the church, backed by woodland and moors.

Much of the village was rebuilt in the mid-18th century for Nathaniel, Lord Crewe, Bishop of Durham, who owned the estate. Many of the buildings, though, have medieval monastic origins. The inn, the Lord Crewe Arms, was once the lodge of the Abbot of Blanchland, and the garden was the abbey cloisters: the boundary with the abbey churchyard is actually the south wall of the monastic church. The inn is said to be haunted by the ghost of Dorothy Forster, Lord Crewe's niece, who rode in disguise to the Tower of London to rescue her brother, imprisoned for his part in the Jacobite uprising of 1715.

The village square was the abbey's outer courtyard, originally entered through the arched gateway at the north end, which now incorporates the village post office. The fountain – locally known as a 'pant' – was put up in 1897 to commemorate Queen Victoria's Diamond Jubilee.

At the end of the bridge go sharp right, between the bridge and a stone building, to the riverside.

Follow the riverside path, going over two ladder stiles. At the signpost turn left, signed 'Blanchland'. Follow the track, which rises and bends left. At the road, cross and follow the raised footpath, back into Blanchland, past the **abbey**.

WHERE TO EAT AND DRINK ⓘ

The **Lord Crewe Arms** offers fine eating in its restaurant, as well as meals in its atmospheric bar. It has a children's room next to the bar and dogs are welcome. The cloister garden is pleasant in warm weather. The **White Monk Tea Rooms** in the village square provide home-made cakes (dogs and children welcome), and there is often an **ice cream van** in the square in the summer months.

This was a Premonstratensian monastery, with white-robed monks – Blanchland is their 'white land'. When Lord Crewe took over the estate, the abbey building was a ruin. He arranged for the chancel, crossing and north transept of the monastic church to be roofed and repaired, so today the church is L-shaped – you enter under the tower into the transept, and turn under the crossing into the main body of the church. On the floor there are grave slabs to some of the abbots, carved with mitres, and foresters, with horns.

Turn right back to the car park at the start of the walk.

WHAT TO LOOK FOR ⓘ

The roadside **wild flowers** in and around Blanchland are worth seeking out. You are likely to spot creeping buttercup, with its large yellow flowers, rough leaves and creeping stems; germander speedwell, which has spikes of bright blue flowers and hairy leaves with serrated edges, and greater stitchwort which has a profusion of white flowers with ten-lobed white petals, that are produced from April to June. In other places you may see the fairy flax, which has white flowers and elliptical leaves, and the bright-yellow heads of the birdsfoot trefoil. Most common of all is cow parsley – sometimes known as Queen Anne's Lace – with its delicate array of tiny white flowers set on long branching stalks.

Causey Arch and the World's Oldest Railway

Through Causey Gill in the footsteps of the railway pioneers of the 18th century.

•DISTANCE•	4 miles (6.4km)
•MINIMUM TIME•	2hrs
•ASCENT / GRADIENT•	394ft (120m) ▲ ▲ ▲
•LEVEL OF DIFFICULTY•	🏃🏃 🏃🏃 🏃🏃
•PATHS•	Mostly on tracks, one short stiff climb
•LANDSCAPE•	Farmland, woodland and industrial relics
•SUGGESTED MAP•	aqua3 OS Explorer 308 Durham & Sunderland
•START / FINISH•	Grid reference: NZ 205561
•DOG FRIENDLINESS•	Off lead for much of walk
•PARKING•	Causey Arch car park, off A6076
•PUBLIC TOILETS•	At car park
•CONTRIBUTOR•	David Winpenny

BACKGROUND TO THE WALK

When the Tanfield Railway was built in 1725 it was reckoned to be the largest civil engineering project since Roman times. It was paid for by a group of local landowners with collieries on their estates – they called themselves the 'Grand Allies'. During the walk you will see some of the enormous earthwork embankments the navvies constructed for the horse-drawn wagons that took coal from the local collieries to wharfs on the River Tyne. Steam trains now run on part of the line, from East Tanfield to Sunniside, with a stop at Causey Arch. Near by is the world's oldest surviving engine shed, built in 1854, where some of the railway's 40 locomotives and carriages can be seen.

Memories of Beamish

The first part of the walk will take you away from the railway towards Beamish Hall, a former home of the Shaftoe family – one of their number, Bobby Shaftoe, attained fame in a nursery song. It was once the headquarters of the National Coal Board, and later an adult education college. It is now used for weddings and conferences. Further along the walk, look out by Beamish Burn for the ghost of a grey lady, said to have been an inhabitant of the hall who hid herself in a trunk to avoid a marriage she did not want, and suffocated. This part of the route follows the Great North Forest Trail, a 65-mile (105km) route from Causey Arch to Marsden Bay near South Shields, that was established as part of an initiative to regenerate urban fringe countryside in the area.

On the Old Track

From East Tanfield you will follow one of several waggon ways that led to Causey Arch. Horses pulled wagons holding four tons of coal along this route above the increasingly steep slopes of the Causey Gill gorge – in many places embankments had to be built to ensure a level route for the wooden rails. Today it is a peaceful path but in its short heyday, from 1725 to the 1740s, the track saw hundreds of waggons, each only 50yds (46m) apart, carry their loads of coal towards the bridge.

The Oldest Arch

Causey Arch is claimed to be the oldest railway bridge in the world. It was built by a local stonemason, Ralph Wood, for the Grand Allies, and at the time it was the largest single-span bridge, 105ft (32m) long and 80ft (24.4m) high. Wood relied on the same building techniques that the Romans used 16 centuries before. After railway activity stopped, the bridge quietly mouldered for almost 200 years until it was restored by Durham County Council in the 1980s. Below the bridge you can see where the Causey Burn was diverted through culverts to enable embankments to be constructed.

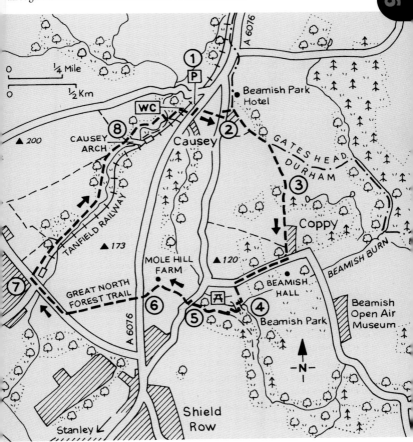

Walk 36 Directions

① From the car park, walk through the 'Exit' archway, left of the toilets. Cross the road and take a signed footpath, left of the bus stop. Cross a stile and go up the field to cross a stile on to a metalled road.

② Turn left. After 200yds (184m) turn right, signed 'Beamish Hall'. Where the concrete track swings right, go straight ahead down a footpath, which brings you to a farm track. Go straight ahead. Where the track forks, bend right. Eventually the track goes through a gateway and into woodland.

③ Descend between houses to a road, opposite **Beamish Hall**. Turn right and follow the road for ½ mile (800m) to the entrance, on the left, to **Beamishburn Picnic Area**. Turn left and follow the lane through the picnic site to a footbridge.

④ Cross the bridge and follow the footpath, which bends right. Where the path forks, continue along the burn side. At a waymarked post turn left, go up steps and go right at a wide crossing track to reach a road. Turn left and then go right, by the Mole Hill Farm sign, marked 'Great North Forest Trail and Causey Arch'.

WHILE YOU'RE THERE ⓘ

Visit **Beamish Open Air Museum**, south east of Beamish Hall, with its reconstruction of an early 20th-century northern town. You can visit period shops, take a lesson in the village school, and even see how the dentist worked, as well as travel on a tram. The Home Farm has traditional farm animals.

---

⑤ Go through a wooden stile beside a gate. Climb the track to a yellow waymark sign on a post. Go left off the track, and follow the path over a wooden stile. Continue with a hedge on your right to another stile. The path beyond curves downhill to a road.

⑥ Cross the road and take the footpath opposite. Ascend the hill, cross a field and descend to another

road. Turn right, and follow the road for ½ mile (800m) to the 'Tanfield Railway' sign.

⑦ Turn right, up the approach road, then go ahead through a gap in the fence. Follow the wagon track alongside the burn, above the gorge, and eventually climb steps to a bench by the start of **Causey Arch**. To avoid the descent into the valley, cross the arch and continue along the path back to the car park.

WHERE TO EAT AND DRINK ⓘ

Opposite Causey Arch is the **Beamish Park Hotel**, which has both a bistro and a dining room. It also runs the **Causey Arch Inn** just across the road which serves a range of bar meals. **Beamish Open Air Museum** offers a wide variety of eating and drinking places – and a sweet factory!

---

⑧ To view the arch, turn left at the bench and go downhill, crossing the burn on a footbridge. Follow the path through woodland and over another footbridge. Go right at the end, then cross another footbridge by a quarry. Do not cross the next footbridge, but bear right, up steps. Turn left at the top and follow the embankment back to the car park.

WHAT TO LOOK FOR ⓘ

In the woodland around the waggon way beside Causey Gill you will be able to spot the **downy birch** tree, typical of the area. You can distinguish it from the silver birch by its rather greyer bark, which has horizontal grooves across it. The leaves are different, too – downy birch leaves are more rounded, and they tend to turn brown rather than yellow in the autumn. The name 'downy birch' comes from the small hairs that cover the tree's twigs.

Derwent Valley's Past

Communism, steel making and Roman remains at Chopwell.

•DISTANCE•	7 miles (11.3km)
•MINIMUM TIME•	2hrs 30min
•ASCENT / GRADIENT•	541ft (165m) ▲ ▲ ▲
•LEVEL OF DIFFICULTY•	👫 👫 👫
•PATHS•	Tracks, field paths and old railway line
•LANDSCAPE•	Woodland and riverside, farmland and industrial remains
•SUGGESTED MAP•	aqua3 OS Explorer 307 Consett & Derwent Reservoir
•START / FINISH•	Grid reference: NZ122579
•DOG FRIENDLINESS•	On lead, except on former railway line
•PARKING•	Roadside parking in Chopwell; follow signs for 'Chopwell Park Car Park'. Car park, itself, opens irregularly
•PUBLIC TOILETS•	None on route
•CONTRIBUTOR•	David Winpenny

BACKGROUND TO THE WALK

It was coal mining that created the village of Chopwell that we see today, with its red-brick buildings and no-nonsense atmosphere – and it was the miners who earned it the name 'Little Moscow' in the 1920s. The coal won from local mines was predominantly used for making coke to stoke the furnaces of the Consett Iron Company. When coal production declined after World War One, many miners were made redundant or put on short-time working. These conditions allowed Communist sympathisers to assume the running of the village. A miners' strike from July 1925 to December 1926 led to accusations of a Communist takeover of the local Labour Party. A national newspaper declared that 'the village is known far and wide as the reddest in England.' Streets were renamed after Marx, Engels and Lenin, and it is said that there were Communist Sunday schools in the village, as well as 'Das Kapital' on the lectern of the local church. For a time the hammer and sickle flag flew over the town hall.

The Cradle of Steel

The area between Blackhall Mill and Derwentcote Ironworks was once the centre of the steel industry in Britain. Steel was made here initially to supply the sword manufacturers of Shotley Bridge, eastwards along the river. Derwentcote, the earliest steel-making furnace to have survived, was built around 1720 and worked until the 1870s. Another furnace at Blackhall Mill lasted until 1834, when a flood washed away its mill dam; the mill was demolished at the beginning of the 20th century. Derwentcote survived, and is now cared for by English Heritage. It is open summer weekends, and contains an interesting explanatory display.

Along the Line

Beyond Derwentcote the walk enters Byerside Wood and then joins the old railway line that now forms the 12½-mile (20.1km) footpath and cycle route of the Derwent Valley Country Park. The route runs from Consett to Gateshead and, at its western end, connects with other

Walk 37

former railway routes, including the Waskerley Way and the Consett and Sunderland Railway Path.

In contrast to the industrial theme of much of the walk, the history of Ebchester stretches much further back in time. Here was the site of the Roman fort of Vindomara, strategically placed where the road we know as Dere Street, which ran from York to the Firth of Forth, crossed the Derwent. Constructed around AD 80, the original timber buildings were later replaced by stone and the fort was finally abandoned in 410. A signboard by the post office shows the layout. It is possible to see its ramparts north of the main road and in the village churchyard. There is a Roman altar in the church tower.

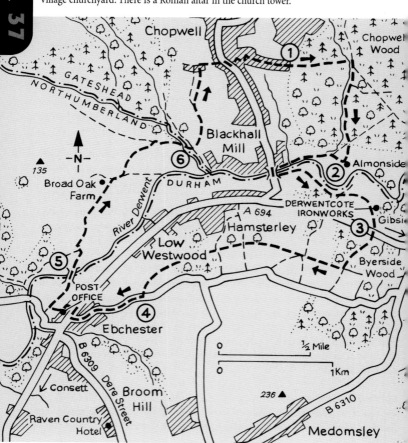

Walk 37 Directions

① Walk up the entrance road to **Chopwell Park**. Turn right past a metal barrier and bear right, past the 'Chopwell Woodland Park' sign. Follow the woodland track, turning right at a crossing track. Pass

another barrier to a metalled area. Turn right and follow the track downhill. Where the woodland ends go over a stile and continue down a fenced path. Enter **Almonside** farmyard through a gate.

② Bear right and follow the track to the road in **Blackhall Mill**. Turn

Walk 37

left, over the bridge. Just after a footpath sign, go left along a field edge, right of the hedge. Follow the fenced riverside path. At a crossing path, turn left, uphill. At the top go sharp left, following waymark signs. Go left of the buildings, over a stile and across the field. Go over two wooden stiles then right. Follow the track uphill, passing **Derwentcote Ironworks**, to the main road.

WHILE YOU'RE THERE
The National Trust's **Gibside Estate** is 4 miles (6.4km) east of Chopwell. Once home to the Bowes-Lyon family, the estate has riverside and forest walks, and a number of ornate buildings, including an 18th-century chapel and 140ft (42.5m) Column of British Liberty. The Gothic Banqueting House is now a holiday cottage.

WHERE TO EAT AND DRINK
In the centre of Chopwell and in Blackhall Mill there are several pubs that serve food. A little up the hill from where the former railway line joins the lane into Ebchester is the **Raven Country Hotel**, which offers both bar meals and a restaurant; children welcome.

③ Cross and take a signed footpath almost opposite. Go over a stile and, at a crossing path, turn right to another stile. Follow the path through woodland to the former railway track. Turn right and follow the track, which crosses another track (barriers at each side) and eventually rises to another barrier on to a metalled lane.

④ Turn right and descend into **Ebchester.** Bend right by the community centre to meet the main road. Cross over and turn right in front of the **post office**. Turn left at the footpath sign beyond. Follow the fence on your left, bend left at

the end beside the wall, then follow the footpath downhill to reach a metalled lane. Turn right along the lane to a footbridge.

⑤ Cross the bridge. The footpath bends right before going straight ahead across the field to a stile. Follow the green lane uphill, pass a farmhouse and follow the track through two gates. Where the main track bears left, go straight ahead. Go through a farm gate, and along the field edge. Go though two gates to a T-junction of tracks.

⑥ Turn left, signposted 'Whinney Leas'. About 300yds (274m) after the farm go right, over a stile, and walk across the field to another stile, hidden in a hedge. Continue up the field to another stile right of the houses, and along a narrow lane. At the end, turn right along the tarmac lane. At the main road turn right and then left, following 'Chopwell Park Car Park' signs back to your car.

WHAT TO LOOK FOR
The 949-acre (384ha) **Chopwell Wood** was once a wild area of oaks and hazel. Much affected by coal mining in the 19th and early 20th centuries, when a railway ran through it, it was taken over by the Forestry Commission in 1919, and largely felled during the two world wars. Restocking from 1952 has left it a mainly coniferous forest, with larch, pine and spruce. There are still patches of earlier broadleaved woodland remaining, however, some of it coppiced. The wood, which became a Woodland Park in 1994 and is managed by Forest Enterprise with the help of a local group, provides habitats for a wide variety of animals, including red squirrels, bats and, in the pools formed in three World War Two bomb craters, great crested newts.

Consett Steel and the River Derwent

Along the banks of the river which first brought steel making to Consett.

Walk 38

•DISTANCE•	3½ miles (5.7km)
•MINIMUM TIME•	1hr 30min
•ASCENT / GRADIENT•	311ft (95m) ▲ ▲ ▲
•LEVEL OF DIFFICULTY•	🚶 🚶 🚶
•PATHS•	River and streamside paths with some roadside walking
•LANDSCAPE•	Pastoral landscapes with reminders of industrial past
•SUGGESTED MAP•	aqua3 OS Explorer 307 Consett & Derwent Reservoir
•START / FINISH•	Grid reference: NZ 085518
•DOG FRIENDLINESS•	Can be off lead for most of walk – look for notices
•PARKING•	Car park off Sandy Lane, off A691
•PUBLIC TOILETS•	Allensford Country Park (may be closed in winter)
•CONTRIBUTOR•	David Winpenny

BACKGROUND TO THE WALK

Even into the late 1970s views of Consett would still be described as 'terrible and magnificent'. As Henry Thorold's *Shell Guide to County Durham*, published in 1980, recorded, 'Vulcan's great forges stand there on the hillside enveloped in steam; cooling towers, cylinders, chimneys, incredible and intimidating.' It was true then – just. But the steel mills of Consett closed in that very year, bringing to an end a story of growth and enterprise that began in 1837 when iron ore was discovered here. The first works opened four years later: by the 1880s the Consett Iron Company, founded in 1864 as a successor to the Derwent Iron Company, employed more than 6,000 people in the rapidly-expanded town. The closure a century later could have devastated Consett. Instead, it has reinvented itself as a place of growing service and manufacturing industry, which also looks back with pride to its history of steel making.

The Derwent Valley

Dividing Northumberland and Durham, this stretch of the River Derwent was the cradle of the northern steel industry. Forge Cottage, just over the footbridge at the start of the walk, indicates that iron working had been long established in the valley. German steel makers, producing fine swords, lived in Shotley Bridge as early as the 1690s – the village later became the fashionable place for the upper middle classes of Consett to live. Shotley Bridge was also a spa – in 1841 it was said that it would soon come to rival Harrogate, Cheltenham and Leamington. As the walk approaches Allensford, there are the remains of a 17th-century ironworks near by.

Allensford Country Park and Woods

Developed by Durham County Council – and right on its northern boundary – Allensford Country Park consists of 14 acres (5.7ha) of riverside grassland. As well as pleasant walks, there are play facilities for children and access for people using wheelchairs. Within the park is Allensford Wood – the walk takes you through part of it. It is semi-natural ancient woodland that is mainly of oak and birch. There has been some recent replanting with native species. A series of trails criss-crosses the wood; the routes are marked with a symbol of a walking man.

Steelworks Site
The section of the walk along Pemberton Road between the road junction (➤ Point ⑤) and the path into the woodland seems quiet today. But until 1980 the whole of the area to your right, now landscaped and grassed, was one of the most industrialised in the country. Here stood one of the British Steel Corporation's mills, its huge buildings alive with noise, smoke and heat. Today it provides an area for recreation and enjoyment, crossed by paths that follow the old railway lines that served the works.

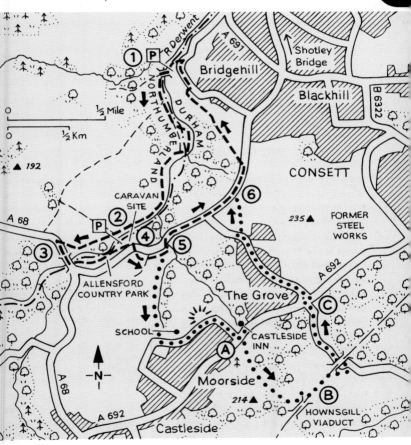

Walk 38 Directions

① From the car park, walk beside the house, following the wall, and bend right to cross the river on a footbridge. Turn left along the river bank and follow it through woodland. Where the path divides stay by the river. Eventually reach an area of beech woodland where the path rises on to a wider track.

Walk 38

WHILE YOU'RE THERE ⓘ

The two 20ft (6m) high *Terris Novalis* **sculptures** stand beside the Consett and Sunderland Railway Path. The huge steel representations of traditional surveyors' instruments, on animal feet, are the work of sculptor Tony Cragg and were manufactured by local craftsmen. They took four years to make and were unveiled in 1997.

Visit **Muggleswick**, 3½ miles (5.6km) west of Consett where, at the farm near the church, are the battlemented remains of a great medieval manor house, built as a grange in the 13th century for the priors of the monastery in Durham. From here they could look over their lands in the Derwent Valley – and today there is a fine view of Consett.

② Follow the track, keeping left when it forks – there are waymarks on this section. The path follows a wire fence, and eventually bears right over a tiny stone bridge skirting a house to reach the **A68**.

③ Turn left down the hill. Go over the road bridge, passing from Northumberland into Durham. Where a road joins from the left, go left through the entrance into **Allensford Country Park**. Bear round to the right, and walk through the grassed riverside area to a car park. Go through the car park to reach a road by the entrance to the caravan site.

④ Go ahead across the road to a waymarked stile in a fence opposite. Follow the path, which goes up two sets of steps. At the top follow the grassy path. Where it divides, bear to the left and follow the winding path into woodland and continue downhill. When you reach a crossing path by a marker post, turn left to the road.

⑤ Turn right and follow the road (take care because it can be busy). It rises through woodland and then passes through a more open area. After ½ mile (800m), pass a road off to the right. In ¼ mile (400m) beyond, look for a footpath that descends on your right to meet the road, by trees.

⑥ Continue to follow the road for 400yds (366m). As the roads rises, take a signed footpath left, downhill into woodland. The path opens out into a track, then becomes a path again. Follow the path for ½ mile (800m) to reach a lane. Turn left here, downhill. At the bottom of the hill turn left again, following the car park sign back to the start of the walk.

WHERE TO EAT AND DRINK ⓘ

There is a refreshment area in **Allensford Country Park**, which also attracts ice cream vans. Otherwise you should head for Shotley Bridge, Castleside or Consett itself, all of which offer plenty of variety for hungry walkers.

WHAT TO LOOK FOR ⓘ

Otters have been spotted in the River Derwent, though you would need to be very lucky to see one. Evidence of their proximity may be found though, including the characteristic footmarks, with their lopsided five-pointed toe marks that turn inwards. Look, too, for the mark of the tail dragging behind the animal. You may also spot places where otters have made mudslides into the water, or where they have scraped up sand into a mound. Adult male otters can be up to 2ft 6in (76cm) long and have a tail – which is thick and tapering and acts as a rudder when the animal is swimming – of up to 20in (50cm). Their short brown fur provides excellent insulation and otters have the ability to close their nostrils and ears to keep out the water.

And on to Splendid Hownsgill Viaduct

This walk takes you to the area's finest railway viaduct and some breathtaking views.
See map and information panel for Walk 38

•DISTANCE•	6¼ miles (10.1km)
•MINIMUM TIME•	2hrs 30min
•ASCENT / GRADIENT•	574ft (175m) ▲▲▲
•LEVEL OF DIFFICULTY•	👥 👥 👥

Walk 39 Directions (Walk 38 option)

At the marker post (Point ⑤ on Walk 38) turn right. Follow the path through the wood. After steps, turn right to follow the path for ½ mile (800m) to a road. Turn left, pass **Moorside School**, and follow the road, which has wide views across the Derwent Valley, as it bends right.

At the main road (Point Ⓐ) turn left. Cross opposite the **Castleside Inn** and follow a signed track towards the **Hownsgill Viaduct**.

It was built in 1858 to carry the Stanhope and Tyne Railway line, across the deep valley formed by Hown's Gill, and it was designed by Thomas Bouch. Each of the 12 arches has a span of 50ft (15m) and the tallest is 150ft (46m) above the valley floor.

At the edge of a pool bear left into woodland. At the top of the first rise turn right towards the viaduct. Keep left where the path branches, then turn left up steps. At a T-junction take the steps on the right, climbing to reach the disused railway line at the end of the viaduct (Point Ⓑ) – it is worth walking on to the viaduct for the views.

Turn left and follow the track, following 'Lanchester Valley Walk' at a fork. The track passes a barrier and reaches a metalled lane. Turn left under the bridge and follow the lane. To your right is the former site of British Steel's Consett works, now landscaped. When you meet a main road (Point Ⓒ), cross and take the road, **Taylors Terrace**, almost opposite. Follow the road and turn left at the mini-roundabout. Almost immediately take a signed footpath right over a stile. Go straight ahead, bearing left where the road on your right bends right. Follow the path down to a road (Point ⑥ on Walk 38).

> **WHAT TO LOOK FOR** ℹ️
> As well as the great spectacle of Hownsgill Viaduct and the former railway lines that criss-cross the area, the smaller reminders of **railway heritage** are everywhere to be seen. They include gradient markers, cast-iron warning plates and even the wheels from old trucks.

Walk 40

The Prince Bishops' Durham

To Durham's castle and cathedral, and along the banks of the River Wear.

•DISTANCE•	2½ miles (4km)
•MINIMUM TIME•	1hr 15min
•ASCENT / GRADIENT•	300ft (91m)
•LEVEL OF DIFFICULTY•	
•PATHS•	City paths and riverside tracks
•LANDSCAPE•	Deep horseshoe-shaped gorge formed by River Wear
•SUGGESTED MAP•	aqua3 OS Explorer 308 Durham & Sunderland; AA Street-by-Street Tyne & Wear
•START / FINISH•	Grid reference: NZ 275424
•DOG FRIENDLINESS•	Off lead, but under close control, on riverside paths
•PARKING•	Prince Bishop car park, off Leazes Road, A690
•PUBLIC TOILETS•	At car park
•CONTRIBUTOR•	David Winpenny

Walk 40 Directions

Leave the car park by the lowest level, by the river. Turn right towards **Elvet Bridge**, originally built around 1170 by Bishop de Puiset and leading to his new suburb of Elvet. Go up the steps at the bridge's right-hand end on to the top. Turn right and walk uphill, then bear left up the steps into **Sadler Street**. After 150yds (137m) turn right up Owengate, signed 'Cathedral and Castle'.

Bear right to the entrance to the castle. Behind the 18th-century gateway is the massive Norman

keep, first built in 1078 on an almost impregnable site on the great spur formed by the River Wear. Guided tours take visitors to the highlights, including the Norman chapel and gallery, and the Black Stair that leads from the medieval Great Hall to the 18th-century state rooms. It was here that the Prince Bishops of Durham – who acted as kings within their area – held court. They raised armies, minted coins, appointed judges and granted charters. Their powers ended in 1832, and the castle was then taken over by the new University of Durham.

Cross **Palace Green** and enter the cathedral by the main door, with its fearsome lion-faced sanctuary ring. The greatest Norman cathedral in England, begun in 1093, Durham has characteristic round pillars with incised geometric carving, as well as the earliest of all Gothic vaults. Durham's saint, Cuthbert, is buried at the east end; near by is the throne of the Prince Bishops, set high

---

WHERE TO EAT AND DRINK ⓘ

As one of the major tourist centres of the north of England, Durham has no shortage of places for refreshment. There is a restaurant in the **cathedral** cloisters, near the Treasury, as well as one on Palace Green. The town centre has pubs of all kinds, many of them popular with students.

above the chancel. Bede, the first English historian, has his tomb in the delicate Galilee Chapel at the west end.

After visiting, leave by the south door into the cloisters. Go straight ahead, turning right to visit the **Treasury**, which holds fine silver, pre-Conquest embroidery and manuscripts, as well as relics of St Cuthbert. As you leave, turn left out of the Treasury and walk along the cloister, then turn right into a passage that emerges into a grassed area called **The College**. Follow the wall on your left as it bends left, and leave by the archway. Turn left.

WHILE YOU'RE THERE ⓘ

Durham Art Gallery and **Durham Light Infantry Regimental Museum** in Aykley Heads have exciting and imaginative displays that are of interest to both adults and children. The art gallery has a changing programme of arts and crafts exhibitions, while the museum tells the story of one of the north east's great army regiments.

Opposite the east end of the cathedral, with its rose window, turn right beside the former church (now the heritage centre) down **Bow Lane**. Bear right to the elegant concrete **Kingsgate Bridge**, put up in 1963 to designs by engineer Ove Arup. Cross the bridge and bear left, to meet the road.

Turn right up **Church Street**. After 100yds (91m), turn right past the war memorial into St Oswald's churchyard. Follow the path as it descends to the river bank, keeping right where it divides. Follow the river, going over a footbridge. On the opposite bank is the little Greek temple, known as the **Count's House** after an early 19th-century Durham resident, Count Boruwlaski, who was 39in (1m) tall.

Pass the end of **Prebends' Bridge**, opened in 1778; one of the cathedral's pinnacles is marooned on the river bank near by. Continue behind the riverside buildings. Just beyond is the classic view of the cathedral, with the former fulling mill (now the Museum of Archaeology) on the opposite bank. Just before the next bridge, go left up steps by the **Coach and Horses** pub on to **Framwellgate Bridge**, put up by Bishop Flambard in 1128.

Turn right over the bridge. Look out on the right for a narrow entry, **Moatside Lane**, signed 'Cathedral and Castle'. Follow the lane, once the main pilgrims' route from the bridge to the cathedral. The lane rises and bends before eventually coming out into **Sadler Street**. Turn left, pass the steps on the right, and then take the next right, **High Street**. At the bottom, go right, back to the car park.

WHAT TO LOOK FOR ⓘ

In **Durham Cathedral Treasury** are fragments of St Cuthbert's coffin. This was probably the one that transported his remains from Holy Island, when the Danes invaded in AD 875, on a journey that ended in Durham in 995. It is incised with figures of saints. Among the other treasures on show is a fearsome sword 35in (89cm) long and weighing more than 2¾lb (1.3kg). This is the Conyers Falchion, presented to each new Bishop of Durham as he formally enters his diocese for the first time. The ceremony takes place on the bridge at Croft-on-Tees. It was near here that, legend says, Sir John Conyers killed the dreaded Sockburn Worm (or dragon) in 1063, for which the bishops awarded him lands. The falchion actually dates from around 1265.

10/6/19. *Lovely walk è Dawn T.*

Through Meadow and Woodland in Weardale

Visit Weardale's prettiest village and stride high to see its best panoramas.

•DISTANCE•	6¾ miles (10.9km)
•MINIMUM TIME•	4hrs
•ASCENT / GRADIENT•	525ft (160m) ▲▲▲
•LEVEL OF DIFFICULTY•	🚶🚶🚶
•PATHS•	Field paths, tracks and country lanes, 5 stiles
•LANDSCAPE•	Riverside meadow, moor and woods
•SUGGESTED MAP•	aqua3 OS Explorer OL31 North Pennines
•START / FINISH•	Grid reference: NY 909380
•DOG FRIENDLINESS•	Should be on leads
•PARKING•	By river at Westgate
•PUBLIC TOILETS•	None on route
•CONTRIBUTOR•	John Gillham

BACKGROUND TO THE WALK

When you go over the 2,000ft (610m) watershed on the moors between Allendale and Weardale you cross into Durham, the land of the Prince Bishops. Like Allendale, upper Weardale has earned its riches from mining, quarrying and farming. Both valleys have the scars to show for it, and they both have the attractive hillside pastures with crazed web-like patterns of the dry-stone walls. However, while Allendale has few villages along its length Weardale has many – charming villages built out of local stone and delightful flower-filled fields that dip into the river.

Powerful Churchmen

Westgate, where the walk starts, marked the western extremity of the Forest Quarter, also known as the Bishops' Park. Here the Prince Bishops hunted for deer, supplying venison for their kitchens. It was said in the 16th century that they hunted with such enthusiasm that the deer population had almost been wiped out. These powerful churchmen reigned from the early Christian times of the Romans, right through to the 1830s. After the Norman King, William Rufus, granted them regal powers they were regarded as second only to the Kings of England and ruled from a palace in Bishop Auckland and their cathedral at Durham.

Green Vistas

The River Wear is your guide as field paths head up the valley to St John's Chapel. This is a larger village with a fine Georgian church and rows of well-to-do cottages. Now you climb the hillsides and turn eastwards along a country road. It may be tarmac, but this 2-mile (3.2km) quiet lane enjoys subtly changing views that are as good as any in the county. Now you can see how green Weardale is, a vivid green that contrasts with the stark high moors of Chapel Fell and Westerhope.

The lane ends and an old cart track takes you up on to the moors, then down into a lonely side valley that once would have reverberated to the sounds of the Middlehope lead mine. The abutment of an old bridge is a relic from an old mine railway that connected Westgate with the mines of Rookhope. Here you follow the stream to the Slit Mines. The shaft, at 585ft (178m), is the one of the deepest in Weardale, while the Slit lead vein at 14 miles (22.5km), is the valley's longest.

Ancient Woodland

The valley, so far, has been a shaly one, but now it narrows and the harder limestone rock surfaces. The river gets playful and tumbles down in a series of waterfalls. You are entering Slit Woods, a Site of Special Scientific Interest (SSSI). The footpath weaves its way through this ancient woodland, a place filled with oaks and rowans, wild strawberries and ransoms. Like many old woods you'll see dog's mercury, wood anemone and wood sorrel, a low creeping perennial with pretty lilac-tinged white flowers. It's a wonderful way into Westgate and a fitting finale for a memorable walk.

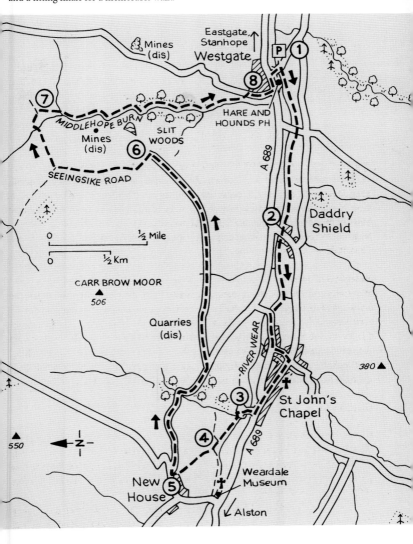

Walk 41 Directions

① From the car park walk out to the road bridge over the **River Wear**. Don't cross but follow the path ahead, which goes across fields alongside the river's south bank. The path crosses a minor road close to a ford and footbridge, then continues by some cottages and across riverside meadows, passing more cottages at **Windyside**.

> **WHAT TO LOOK FOR** ⓘ
>
> You may notice the purple **fluorspar** crystals scattered around the mines' washing floors or sparkling on the stream bed. It was considered a waste product of lead mining when that industry was in full swing, but later fluorspar was found to be useful, and mined in its own right, as a fusion agent in the steel manufacturing industry.

② On reaching the main road at **Daddry Shield** turn right, then left, over the crash barrier and down to the Wear's south bank again. This new path stays closer to the river than before. Turn left on meeting a country lane and follow it into the village of **St John's Chapel**. Turn right along the main street and pass through the village.

③ At the far side of the village, turn right along the signed footpath that tucks under the old railway bridge and crosses a footbridge over the river. Beyond the crossing turn left through a gap stile to follow a path close to the north bank. Ignore the next footbridge, but instead head for the farmhouse, which should be rounded on the left.

④ Follow a grassy enclosed path raking diagonally across hillside pasture to reach a high country lane above the hamlet of **New House**.

⑤ Turn right along the lane then, after about ¾ mile (1.2km), take the higher left-hand fork which traverses the southern side of **Carr Brow Moor** with its disused quarries and mine shafts.

⑥ At its terminus turn left up the walled **Seeingsike Road** (track). Turn right at a junction of tracks and descend into **Middlehope Cleugh**. Conveniently placed stones allow a crossing of the river.

⑦ Turn right again to follow **Middlehope Burn**'s east bank, past a series of lead mines. The path enters **Slit Woods** and comes out by a mill and some cottages on the outskirts of **Westgate**.

⑧ The lane leads to the main road where you turn left, then right past the **Hare and Hounds** pub, back to the car park.

> **WHERE TO EAT AND DRINK** ⓘ
>
> **Atholl's Restaurant** at the Cross Keys in Eastgate stands out well above all others. Here the chef, Atholl Graham, produces tasty meals like venison served with a port wine and blackberry sauce.

> **WHILE YOU'RE THERE** ⓘ
>
> Visit the **Weardale Museum** and **High House Chapel** at Ireshopeburn. The folk museum's displays include the kitchen of a farmer or lead miner as it would have been in the 17th to 19th centuries, a collection of local crystallised minerals and exhibitions of local history. Learn about the Weardale railways and about the visits of preacher John Wesley. High House Chapel (founded 1760) is the oldest Methodist chapel in the world in continuous use. Open afternoons May to September except Monday and Tuesday.

High on Byerhope Bank

Taking to the high moors of Hexhamshire.

•DISTANCE•	5 miles (8km)
•MINIMUM TIME•	3hrs
•ASCENT / GRADIENT•	656ft (200m) ▲▲▲
•LEVEL OF DIFFICULTY•	🚶🚶 🚶🚶 🚶🚶
•PATHS•	Stony tracks and generally well-defined paths, 3 stiles
•LANDSCAPE•	High moor and rough pasture
•SUGGESTED MAP•	aqua3 OS Explorer OL31 North Pennines
•START / FINISH•	Grid reference: NY 860453
•DOG FRIENDLINESS•	Sheep country: dogs should be under close control
•PARKING•	In Allenheads village centre
•PUBLIC TOILETS•	By heritage centre
•CONTRIBUTOR•	John Gillham

BACKGROUND TO THE WALK

The hills of Hexhamshire are wild and windy and, if there's a hint of cloud in the skies, they're dark, dramatic and brooding. In summer sun the drama is brought into colour by the vivid purple blooms of the bell heather. For ramblers in the Tyne and Allen valleys Hexhamshire offers walks both long and short; walks where you can see to far horizons and stride out with the aroma of that heather wafting in the winds. Allenheads is a good place to start. As its name suggests, this village lies at the end of the Allen Valley, where the green fields give way to the high moors.

Prosperous Lead Mining Area

Like many villages in these parts Allenheads' prosperity grew and declined with the lead mining industry, but just about keeps a foot in the 21st century with tourism. At one time the village had a population of over 1,000: now it's not much over 100. Cottages line the river, with an inn, heritage centre and café half-hidden by conifer plantations.

This route heads in the Rookhope direction, on to the moors of Byerhope. A stony track, the course of the Broad Way, takes you along the fringes of the moor, overlooking Allendale. The track was built initially to carry ore and supplies between the lead mining villages but has now been surfaced for the Land Rovers of grouse shooting parties. The profuse heather makes these some of the best shooting moors in England.

Beyond some quarries the track winds around to Byerhope, which in past centuries was a thriving village of farms and smallholdings owned by lead miners. Like many of the families of Allenheads, the Byerhope miners were involved in a bitter strike in 1849 with W B Lead over a time and motions study that engineer, Sir Thomas Sopwith, had imposed on them. There was fiery talk of tormenting blacklegs to their graves, but the strike was eventually broken. Those who held out were banished from working the mines again and were forced to leave, many to America. At Byerhope, today, there's just one inhabited cottage and a few crumbled ruins.

The route leaves the Broad Way on the hillsides beneath High Haddock Stones. A grassy zig-zag path offers pleasing prospects across Allendale to Knockshield Moor and Killhope

Walk 42

Law. Past a terrace of colourfully painted cottages you come down to the river and follow it past Peasmeadows and along banks of heather, rowan and bilberry. The bright yellow marsh marigolds grow from riverside rocks. Here I saw dippers trying to dive for insects but being hampered by a frolicking weasel jumping from rock to rock with an elusive meal on its mind. And so the river takes you back to the outskirts of Allenheads, where the back road eases you past the strangely named hamlet of Dirt Pot to the village centre.

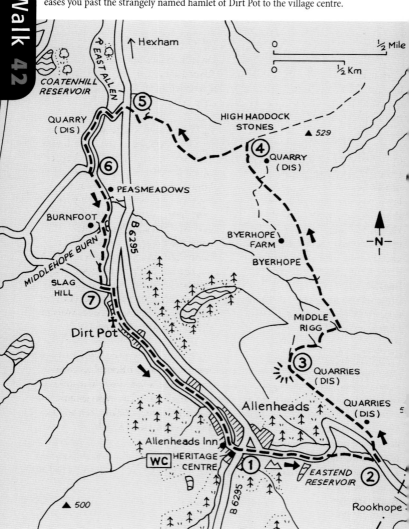

Walk 42 Directions

① From the front of the **heritage centre** head east to the **B6295** road which you cross to follow the lane

signposted to Rookhope. This climbs steeply out of the valley between spruce plantations. At a sharp left-hand bend beyond **Eastend Reservoir**, leave the road and go over a step stile on a path

Walk 42

signed 'Rookhope Road'. Trackless, but guided by a wall on the right, the path climbs westwards across two fields of rough pasture and over two stiles.

② After cutting a corner the path rejoins the road and arrives at an old quarry high on the moors. Turn left along the road for a few paces, then follow a stony track at the right-hand side. This traces the moorland rim above Allenheads, which now hides in the forest.

③ After passing a quarry and huge cairn (good views of Allendale) the track turns right then meanders around **Middle Rigg** before turning sharp left to pass the old ruins of **Byerhope** hamlet.

④ Beyond the occupied **Byerhope Farm**, at **High Haddock Stones**, the track swings right again, away from the valley. Here you leave it. A waymarker post, the first of many, highlights the bridleway wanted. This clear grooved grassy path makes a circuitous descent into

Allendale, where you'll notice the quarries of Swinhope and the Coatenhill Reservoir. After passing some old grassed-over quarry workings the bridleway descends to a gate by a row of colourful terraced cottages on the main valley road.

⑤ Across the road go straight on, down a minor lane, which fords the **River East Allen**; fortunately, there's a wooden footbridge on the right to help you across.

⑥ Where the road bends right uphill at **Peasmeadows**, leave it and go down the cottage's drive, beyond which a riverside path begins. Ignore the first bridge across the river and stay with the path past **Burnfoot**. Go across a footbridge over **Middlehope Burn**, then continue though a pleasing little ravine of heather and bilberry. As it approaches lead mining spoil heaps the path gets sketchy. The easiest course is to climb to the brow of the bank on the right and follow this to the road near **Slag Hill**.

⑦ Turn left down the road to recross the **East Allen**, then turn right at the T-junction. The quiet lane leads back into **Allenheads**, past the hamlet of **Dirt Pot** and the old Presbyterian chapel.

W a l k 4 3

Industrial Rookhope

The lead mining relics in this fascinating area inspired a 20th-century poet.

•DISTANCE•	5¼ miles (8.4km)
•MINIMUM TIME•	2hrs
•ASCENT / GRADIENT•	508ft (155m) ▲▲ ▲▲ ▲
•LEVEL OF DIFFICULTY•	👫 👫 👫
•PATHS•	Tracks and field paths, one steep climb. Use former railway tracks as embankment may be unstable in places
•LANDSCAPE•	Former lead mining area with reminders of industrial past
•SUGGESTED MAP•	aqua3 OS Explorer 307 Consett & Derwent Reservoir
•START / FINISH•	Grid reference: NY 924430
•DOG FRIENDLINESS•	Can be off lead on much of trackbed
•PARKING•	Parking area beside Rookhope Arch, west of village
•PUBLIC TOILETS•	None on route
•CONTRIBUTOR•	David Winpenny

BACKGROUND TO THE WALK

Rookhope – its name means 'valley of the rooks' – is today a small, remote Weardale village. But it has a long and fascinating history. By 1153, when King Stephen granted a licence to mine for lead and iron, it was known as Rykhup. In the 14th century the local farmers combined agriculture with searching out the lead on the stream banks. The Rookhope farmers were generally free from the cattle raids that plagued their counterparts further north, but a famous raid of 1569 into Weardale ended with the raiders cornered in the Rookhope Valley, where a pitched battle resulted in victory for the Weardale men. Their exploits were recorded in the 24-verse ballad *Rookhope Ryde*.

A Bustling Town

Nineteenth-century Rookhope was a great contrast to the rest of its history. Under the influence of the Blackett family, the Weardale Iron Company and then the Weardale Lead Company, Rookhope became a bustling, noisy, industrial town, dedicated to winning minerals out of the ground in the surrounding hills. In its heyday its population approached 1,000, with ten shops, several churches and chapels, an Institute and generous sports fields. The mine owners maintained a paternalistic but benevolent eye on their workforce. There were still mines operating in the Rookhope area into the 1990s, mainly for fluorspar.

There are still many reminders of Rookhope's industrial past in the area – and the most expressive is the great arch near the start of the walk. It is the only surviving fragment of a row of six such arches that carried the 2-mile (3.2km) flue, known as Rookhope Chimney, from the smelt works at Lintzgarth across the valley. After crossing the river, the flue ran for 1 mile (1.6km) underground and ½ mile (800m) up the hillside. Its purpose was to cool the gases from the smelting floor, in which there was much vaporised lead. The lead was deposited on the walls of the flue, and was either scraped off or washed away with water flowing along the tunnel into special 'fume tanks'. The car park is the site of one of them.

The Rookhope area's mining relics were a formative influence on the poet W H Auden (1907–73). Lead mining fascinated Auden as a boy, and a visit he made to Rookhope in

Walk 43

1919, when he was 12, proved a life-changing experience. He suddenly saw these derelict remains as symbols of mankind's lost beliefs. His poems of the 1920s contain many references to the industry, including technical terms that must have puzzled many of his readers. Auden himself was in no doubt of the importance of his Rookhope experience 'There in Rookhope,' he wrote in *New Year Letter*, 'I was first aware of self and not-self, Death and Dread.'

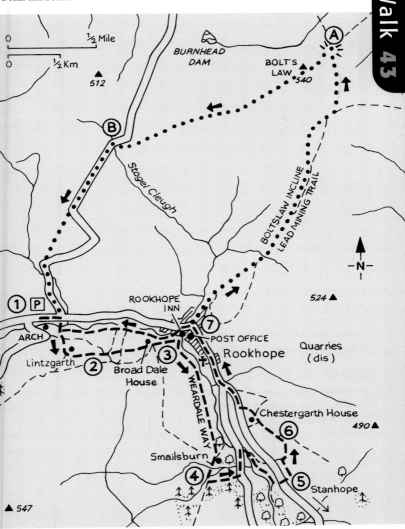

Walk 43 Directions

① Walk towards **Rookhope**. Opposite the Blanchland road go right, over a stile and footbridge.

Go ahead, bending left when past the white building, then right on to a track. Go through a gate, and left, uphill. After a cattle grid bear left when the track divides. Go through two metal gates to a white house.

Walk 43

② Just beyond, take a path left then descend and go through a gate in the wall on your right. Cross the field to a stile, then on through a gate towards a stile by farm buildings. Pass in front of them to a wooden stile. Head downhill towards the village, to a ladder stile.

WHERE TO EAT AND DRINK ℹ️

In Rookhope the **Rose and Crown** near the church offers meals and real ale (dogs allowed). The **Rookhope Inn** also has real ale, and home-cooked food. Both provide a pleasant place to stop and children are welcome, but check at the Rose and Crown when you arrive.

---

③ After the stile walk past buildings and turn right along the track for ¾ mile (1.2km), going through three gates, then through a farmyard with two more. Follow the track beyond, uphill, to where it bends left.

④ Turn left. As the track disappears continue downhill to a stile. Turn left along the road. Just after a small lay-by go right over a stile, signed 'Weardale Way'. Cross the footbridge and climb the path opposite, bearing right. Walk through the field, go over a stile then uphill to a gate on the ridge.

⑤ Cross the lane and go through a gate opposite. The track curves left then disappears. Go towards the left of the buildings, then bear left keeping beside the wall. At the field end go right, over a stile, then head left to a gate by the house.

⑥ Go through the gate and up steps on your right to a hand gate into the field. Turn left, behind the house, go though a gate and cross the field bearing slightly left to another gate. Walk behind the buildings and at the end take a wooden gate to the left of a metal farm gate. Pass the large farm building then go downhill to a stile on to a lane. Turn right, then right again at the junction into **Rookhope** village.

WHILE YOU'RE THERE ℹ️

Visit nearby **Stanhope**, called the Capital of Weardale. In the churchyard is the fossilised stump of a 250 million-year-old tree. In Heathery Burn Cave near by, the possessions of a Bronze-Age family (now in the British Museum) were discovered in 1850. For today's visitors there is an open-air swimming pool and pleasant walks beside the River Wear.

---

⑦ Pass the post office and the **Rookhope Inn**, then take a signed path, left. Cross the bridge and turn right along the track at the 'Rookhope Trails' sign. The path ascends to a higher track. Continue over a stile and ahead, past the nursery. After a gate and a wooden stile, turn right over the footbridge, go over the stile and turn left on the road back to the start.

WHAT TO LOOK FOR ℹ️

From Rookhope to Smailsburn farm the walk follows the route of the former **railway line** built by the Weardale Coal and Iron Company. The route continues beyond Smailsburn for another 3 miles (4.8km) to Westgate where it originally joined the Wear Valley line. According to a late 19th-century survey, the line was 'used for the conveyance of coal, limestone, lead, &c. Coal for the village, smelt-mill, and Westgate; limestone from the quarry of the Weardale Coal and Iron Company to their iron-works, and lead from the mines to the smelt-mill, and thence to the market.' The mines and quarries around the Rookhope Burn valley also had their own branches, some of them of smaller gauge.

Up the Incline

This moorland extension loop takes you up to Bolt's Law and past more of Rookhope's mining history.

See map and information panel for Walk 43

•DISTANCE•	8½ miles (13.7km)
•MINIMUM TIME•	2hrs
•ASCENT / GRADIENT•	1,361ft (415m) ▲▲▲
•LEVEL OF DIFFICULTY•	🚶🚶🚶

Walk 44 Directions (Walk 43 option)

Opposite **Rookhope Post Office** (Point ⑦) turn right on the signed uphill track. This is **Boltslaw Incline**, constructed in 1846. It linked the plant of the Wearside Lead Company on the hillside to the railway line. Wagons were hauled up the incline by a stationary steam engine – you will pass the remains of the engine house at the top of the rise, where it joined the line that looped east towards Consett – once England's highest standard-gauge line.

WHILE YOU'RE THERE ⓘ

Frosterley, down the valley from Stanhope, is an industrial village with rows of terraced houses. Quarrying has been carried out here since at least the Middle Ages for black limestone, rich in fossils, that will take high polish. Known as Frosterley Marble, it was used inside many great churches in the north, including Durham Cathedral and the chapel at Auckland Castle.

Follow the track past Lead Mining Trail and C2C National Cycle Network markers. This 140-mile (225km) route links the Irish and North seas. Starting on the Lake District coast, it crosses the North Pennines and ends at Sunderland or on Tyneside. Where the track bends left, follow the signs towards Consett and Sunderland. Go through a metal gate, still following the C2C cycleway. Continue through spoil heaps as the path levels out, passing ruins on your left. About ½ mile (800m) beyond, before a sheepfold, turn left across moorland.

Go over a waymarked stile beside a large post and go straight ahead. At the second waymarked post (Point Ⓐ), from which there are wide views, turn left up the track towards the hilltop. Go through a gate to the triangulation point on **Bolt's Law**: the view includes Burnhead Dam below. Return to the track and continue downhill. After ½ mile (800m) go through a wooden gate. Cross a track and continue on a faint path, towards a bend in the road ahead. Pass a Lead Mining Trail waymark to reach the road by a signpost (Point Ⓑ). Turn left. Where the road bends sharply left, follow the Lead Mining Trail sign straight on downhill, to rejoin the road, and continue downhill to the junction near the burn. Turn right, back the start of Walk 43.

Walk 45

Hamsterley Forest

Take an easy hike through the Christmas trees of Durham's largest forest.

•DISTANCE•	4½ miles (7.2km)
•MINIMUM TIME•	2hrs 30min
•ASCENT / GRADIENT•	600ft (183m) ▲ ▲ ▲
•LEVEL OF DIFFICULTY•	🚶 🚶 🚶
•PATHS•	Forest track and clear paths, no stiles
•LANDSCAPE•	Forest
•SUGGESTED MAP•	aqua3 OS Explorer OL31 North Pennines or leaflet (small fee) *A Guide to Hamsterley Forest* from visitor centre
•START / FINISH•	Grid reference: NZ 093312
•DOG FRIENDLINESS•	Well-behaved dogs can run free in forest
•PARKING•	Large pay car park near visitor centre
•PUBLIC TOILETS•	By visitor centre
•CONTRIBUTOR•	John Gillham

Walk 45 Directions

The Grove in Hamsterley was home to the Surtees family, who farmed here and used the estate for hunting. One of the family Robert Smith Surtees (1805–64), created the character John Jorrocks, a fox-hunting cockney grocer who became Master of the Foxhounds. His popular articles appeared regularly in the *New Sporting Magazine* and in the novel *Jorrocks' Jaunts and Jollities*.

WHERE TO EAT AND DRINK ⓘ

There's a **café** near the visitor centre, but if you're looking for a hearty bar meal try the 18th-century **Duke of York Country Inn** on the A68 at Fir Tree, near Crook. The comfortable coaching inn is rightly proud of its furniture, some items were made by Yorkshire woodcarver, Robert Thompson. The blackboard menu is varied and includes vegetarian dishes. It's a free house with many fine ales including Black Sheep. There's also a children's play area.

The Grove is still an attractive place today, sited in a clearing by the confluence of the Euden and Spurlswood becks and surrounded by some of the oldest trees in the region. However, when the Forestry Commission purchased the estate in 1927, they created Durham's most extensive plantation, Hamsterley Forest, covering over 5,000 acres (2,025ha) of the Bedburn and Ayhope valleys. Extending well into those fragrant heather moors, the Sitka spruce, larches and Scots pines engulfed the estate. Though the conifers are interspersed with broadleaved trees, including 62 acres (25ha) of oakwood, many find the spread unattractive and at one time it was suggested that wildlife would be decimated. However, around 150,000 visitors come here every year to enjoy the scenery and walk the waymarked trails. The quiet observant ones are able to study the abundant wildlife – the shy roe deer and the red squirrel, or up in the tree boughs, the woodpeckers and nuthatches.

Walk 45

This route follows one of the Forestry Enterprise's waymarked trails. Like all the walks it begins from the trailhead notice board north of the main car park and close to the visitor centre. You will be following the orange waymarkers around the Bedburn Valley.

Head south past the car park, turn right alongside **Bedburn Beck**. Follow the track that comes in from the right, and cross the bridge spanning the beck. The track angles away from the beck and climbs through **Windy Bank Wood**. At a junction of tracks turn left, then climb right, on a dirt path through the trees to reach another forestry road where you turn right. Go straight across the tarmac lane encountered and continue along the forestry track on the other side.

Where the forestry road turns sharp left, leave it for a woodland path descending to a forest track where you turn left. An orange waymarker highlights the next path on the right, which descends through the trees re-crossing the tarred lane before meeting and running alongside the forest toll road.

Use the road bridge to cross the beck, then follow the path to the right on the other side. This traces the stream behind the Grove car park. Don't cross the bridge to the car park but continue along the track that swings right through the trees before climbing in a northerly direction. You are now following an old coach road from Barnard Castle to Wolsingham, which went high over Cabin Hill at Doctor's Gate. Cattle drovers would also have used this ancient route.

The stony highway escapes the conifers, on one side at least, and there are views on the right, down to the valley pastures of Middle Redford. The place is scattered with rowans and sycamore, with heather on the verges and there's an old ruin on the left.

At the far end of a large clearing on the right the route turns off the forest road but stays with the old drove road. This heads north east to the ruins of **Metcalf's House**, formerly an inn and once a popular resting place for coaches and drovers. There are picnic tables next to the ruins for those who would dwell here, but alas you'll have to bring your own beer.

The path now heads east, parallel to the banks of **Ayhope Beck**, a pleasing stream scampering over mossy rocks and by some fine stands of Scots pine.

The path rejoins the toll road at **Low Redford**. After following this for a short way take the left fork, a tarmac drive passing some forestry cottages before degenerating into a track. The orange route soon diverts off the drive along a path to the right. Near the eastern edge of the forest this path descends right, and goes down some steps to emerge at the **visitor centre**.

Cow Green Reservoir and the Tees

Discover the valley of the upper Tees as it meanders through the remote hillscapes of Widdybank Fell.

Walk 46

•DISTANCE•	8 miles (12.9km)
•MINIMUM TIME•	5hrs
•ASCENT / GRADIENT•	525ft (160m) ▲▲▲
•LEVEL OF DIFFICULTY•	🚶🚶 🚶🚶 🚶
•PATHS•	Roads tracks and well-defined paths, 2 stiles
•LANDSCAPE•	Moorland and rough pasture
•SUGGESTED MAP•	aqua3 OS Explorer OL31 North Pennines
•START / FINISH•	Grid reference: NY 810309
•DOG FRIENDLINESS•	Dogs should be kept on leads
•PARKING•	Car park at Cow Green
•PUBLIC TOILETS•	Below car park
•CONTRIBUTOR•	John Gillham

BACKGROUND TO THE WALK

Cow Green was a sleepy backwater of Upper Teesdale, a remote farming and lead-mining community. Here the Tees, barely down from its birthplace on the windswept expanses of Cross Fell, meandered in a wide heather and marsh basin. There were two famous views: the first, the Teesdale Wheel, where the Tees flowed in a huge circle, and the second, Cauldron Snout, lay just beyond, where the river thundered down dolerite cliffs in one of Britain's most spectacular waterfalls.

Unique Plants

It had long been known that the area was of great interest to botanists, and teams had often made pilgrimages here to see the unique collection of arctic alpine plants. In the 1950s and 60s there were rumours. Darlington needed more water and they had their eyes on Cow Green. Conservationists were up in arms. Letters were sent to *The Times*; scientists from all over the world protested that the site was just too valuable. Wainwright joined the protesters with the first edition of his little green *Pennine Way Companion*. He declared that to flood this land would be a desecration. A public enquiry was set up. Cow Green was chosen. Scientists and volunteers were allowed access to the site before flooding in order to remove specimens of the rare species and replant them above the proposed water line. By 1970 the dam had been built, the waters rose, slowly but surely, above the Teesdale Wheel until it was no more, and to the top of the concrete. Only Cauldron Snout survived.

What made Cow Green so special? It is believed to be the harsh climate and the presence of sugar limestone, a rock that has been baked by the intrusion of molten whin sill, the other predominant rock of the region. Behaving and looking like sand, its soils support a multitude of species, including spring gentian, dog violet, thyme, harebell, shrubby cinquefoil, primrose, and spring sandwort. The Teesdale violet only grows on Widdybank Fell, and tracts of juniper helped the survival of a large bird population.

Walk 46

Over the Fell to the River

The area is part of the Moor House–Upper Teesdale National Nature Reserve, which encompasses 18,285 acres (7,400ha) of the headwaters of the Tees. English Nature, who manage the reserve with the estate owners, have waymarked a nature trail that will form the latter part of this long walk. First though, the route heads east over Widdybank Fell to join the Tees downriver. It's a fascinating course, across the fields of lonely Widdybank Farm, through the meandering, ever tightening, valley of the Tees and between the jumbled rocks of Cronkley Fell and Falcon Clints. Each corner brings a new view, but each corner takes you further from civilisation, into a world of dark and dramatic heather hillscapes. The Tees is wide and shallow, and splashes over a bouldery bed. The path sometimes gets nearer to the river than you would like and you find yourself hopping over boulders smoothed by the boots of a thousand Pennine wayfarers.

On To Thundering Cauldron Snout

Then you come to Cauldron Snout. Cow Green Reservoir hasn't stopped it foaming and it still thunders down those dolerite cliffs. An exciting path scrambles up by its side and comes to that dam and disappointment. Back in civilisation a hard stony track, then an even harder tarred road take you around the reservoir shores. If its spring your mood may lighten if you can just find the tiny blue blooms of the spring gentian.

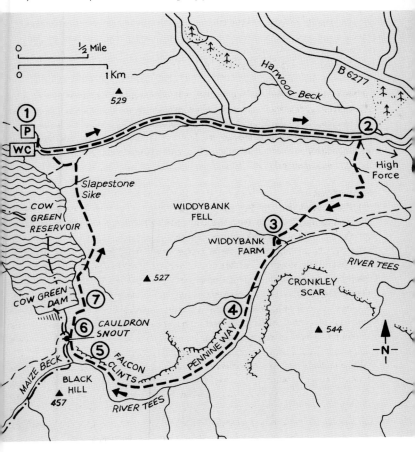

Walk 46

Walk 46 Directions

① From the car park walk back along the road across the desolate **Widdybank Fell** and over the watershed, where the wide green sweep of Harwood Beck's valley comes into view. Go ahead at the junction with the Harwood road.

WHERE TO EAT AND DRINK ⓘ

Try the **Langdon Beck Hotel**, which you pass on the way to the start of the walk. This welcoming free house country pub is child friendly and well-behaved dogs are allowed. The menu features traditional bar meals alongside dishes such as lamb Auvergne.

---

② As the road approaches the river, leave it for a signposted path on the right, which follows the track to **Widdybank Farm**. The winding track heads for the rocks of **Cronkley Scar** which lies on the far banks of the River Tees.

③ Through the farmyard of Widdybank the path goes over a stile by a gate and veers left across rough pasture to join the **Pennine Way** by the banks of the **Tees**.

④ Across grassy plains at first, the path threads through a tightening gorge, eventually to be squeezed by the cliffs and boulders of **Falcon Clints** on to a bouldery course close to the river. Briefly a grassy plain develops and the path, sometimes stony and traversing heather and sometimes crossing marshy areas

using duckboards, continues into the wild North Pennine recesses. Across the river you'll see warning signs posted by the army to keep you from straying on to their firing range. Usually the guns are a long way off and all is calm.

⑤ The valley of **Maize Beck** comes in from behind Black Hill in the west, and the route comes to the foot of the impressive cataract of **Cauldron Snout**. Here the path becomes a bit of a scramble up rocks beside the falls – take care.

⑥ At the top of the falls you are confronted with the huge **Cow Green dam**. Here the Pennine Way turns left to cross a footbridge over the Tees but your route continues along a lane, which climbs to the top right of the dam.

⑦ The lane continues above the eastern shores of the reservoir. You're now on the nature trail and there are numbered attractions. There are no interpretation notices – annoying if you didn't bring the explanatory leaflet (available from local tourist information centres). Beyond a gate across the road leave the tarmac and turn left along the track, which returns to the car park.

WHILE YOU'RE THERE ⓘ

Take a look at that other waterfall, **High Force**, which can be reached on a short walk from a roadside lay-by north of the Bowlees Visitor Centre. Here the Tees falls in one drop 70ft (21m) into a deep pool in a gorge beneath dolerite cliffs.

WHAT TO LOOK FOR ⓘ

On the south side of Slapestone Sike you'll notice a spoil heap and the concrete cap of a mineshaft. The remains are from a **baryte** (barium sulphate) **mine**, which operated until the 1950s. The mineral was used in the manufacture of paper and paint. Its high density also made it useful as a drilling mud (lubricant and coolant) for oil rigs. Near the beck you may also spot the white, star-like flowers of the toxin-loving spring sandwort.

Barnard Castle

Walking round and about old Barney.

•DISTANCE•	4¼ miles (6.8km)
•MINIMUM TIME•	2hrs 30min
•ASCENT / GRADIENT•	165ft (50m) ▲ ▲▲ ▲▲
•LEVEL OF DIFFICULTY•	‹‹ ‹‹ ‹‹
•PATHS•	Town streets and good paths, 6 stiles
•LANDSCAPE•	Riverside and market town
•SUGGESTED MAP•	aqua3 OS Explorer OL31 North Pennines
•START / FINISH•	Grid reference: NZ 051163
•DOG FRIENDLINESS•	Dogs should be on leads
•PARKING•	Pay-and-display car park at end of Queen Street between Galgate and Newgate
•PUBLIC TOILETS•	On Market Place
•CONTRIBUTOR•	John Gillham

BACKGROUND TO THE WALK

Approach Barnard Castle from Bowes and you'll see the imposing nature of its fortress, which tops a bold 80ft (25m) crag and towers above the River Tees. The castle was built in 1112 for Bernard de Baliol, whose father Guy had fought side by side with William the Conqueror at the Battle of Hastings. The Baliols would become a powerful force in the north, and John Baliol, with a little help from Edward I, would become King of Scotland in 1292. In the same century the little town that had grown around the castle was granted a charter for a market. The medieval layout of streets, yards and back alleys still exists today and many of the older buildings have survived. Our look around the town, affectionately known as old Barney, will reveal this to the full.

Riverside Woods

The walk begins with back alleys that take you past St Mary's Parish Church, founded in the 12th century. You continue down to Demesnes, open parkland by the Tees, where springs once supplied the town with drinking water. On the leisurely walk by the Tees you'll see grey marble riverbeds, a stone that has supplied building material for the locals, including a fine font in St Mary's. The pretty riverside woods may also reveal beds of anemones and primroses. Through the trees Egglestone Abbey appears. You may have seen it in one of Turner's paintings.

Abbey Bridge takes you across the river, which hereabouts has formed a deep gorge, and gives you a closer look at the old abbey, founded around 1196 by Ralph de Multon for the Premonstratensian order. After the dissolution of the monasteries the abbey was sold to Robert Streeley, who converted the cloisters into a house, which has long since been in ruins. Today the best-preserved part of the abbey is the church, which stands on a grassy knoll above the river. As you make your approach you will be impressed by the elegant double-lancet windows and its unusual mullioned east window.

A quiet lane takes the route past Bow Bridge, a 17th-century packhorse bridge across Thorsgill Beck. Just beyond this you're back on field paths above the Tees. Two majestic

Walk 47

buildings come in and out of view over the treetops. One is the Bowes Museum (➤ While You're There) and the other, Barnard Castle School.

And so you come back to old Barney, over the footbridge to Thorngate. At the top the route heads for the castle. A visit here will inform you about its colourful history. It was captured by one of the Prince Bishops of Durham and in 1569, during the Rising of the North against Elizabeth I, it was subjected to an 11-day siege. The damage inflicted made rebuilding necessary, though the round keep, added in the 14th-century, survived.

Beyond the castle you come to Galgate, a wide street that used to be called Gallowgate, a place where the gallows stood. It was also the course of a Roman road linking forts at Bowes and Binchester. Market Place on the right is the commercial centre of Barnard Castle. Here you'll see the former Kings Head Inn, now called the Charles Dickens, where Dickens stayed while researching for his novel, *Nicholas Nickleby* (1839). At the end of Market Place you come to the octagonal Market Cross building of 1747. They used to hold town council meetings and courts on the first floor and use the lower part as a lock-up.

Last but not least on this journey through history is a street known as The Bank. Among the fine old buildings you'll come across is the town's most famous, the 4-storey 16th-century Blagraves House, now a restaurant. Oliver Cromwell is supposed to have stayed here during his visit to the town in 1648.

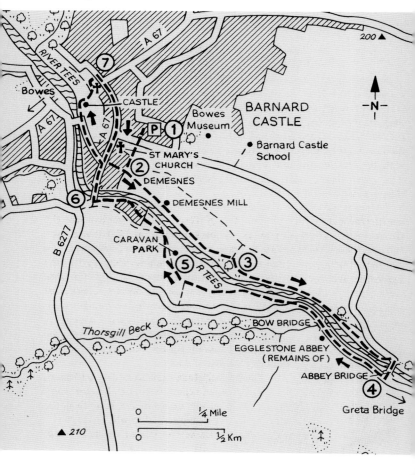

Walk 47 Directions

① From the car park go through the passageway signposted for the river. Go across **Newgate Street** and continue through another little ginnel, which leads through the churchyard of St Mary's and then out on to the riverside parkland of **Demesnes**.

WHILE YOU'RE THERE

When John Bowes married French actress Josephine Coffin-Chevalier they had Jules Pellechet to oversee the building of a 'French château', on Newgate Street in Barnard Castle, to house their immense collection of arts and treasures. Here, at the **Bowes Museum**, you can view elegant furniture and ceramics; paintings by Canaletto, Goya and Turner; extensive gardens and a life-sized silver, musical swan.

② Here turn left along a stony path, which angles down to the river. It passes **Demesnes Mill**, then follows the north bank of the Tees, with the river on your right.

③ You pass (quickly if the wind is in the wrong direction) the sewage works. Ignore the upper left fork of two paths and stay by the river to enter pretty woodland, which allows glimpses of the remains of **Egglestone Abbey** on the far banks.

WHERE TO EAT AND DRINK

There are lots of pubs, cafés and restaurants in the town. If you want a restaurant meal and are willing to splash out a bit, follow Oliver Cromwell into **Blagraves House**. For a bar meal in the nearby countryside try the **Morritt Arms** at Greta Bridge. It's a welcoming old coaching inn. In summer you can eat in the gardens: in winter there's a fire in the Dickens Bar. Children and dogs welcome.

Go through the gate on to the road and turn right over **Abbey Bridge**.

④ Turn right at the junction on the far side of the bridge, then go left up the access track to view the abbey. Return to the road and follow it left, to pass **Bow Bridge**. A squeeze stile in the hedge on the right marks the start of the path along the south bank of the Tees. On the approach to a caravan park the path crosses fields and veers slightly away from the river.

⑤ Turn right along a surfaced track, down to the **caravan park** and take the second drive on the left, which eventually leads to the continuation of the riverside path.

WHAT TO LOOK FOR

The **County Bridge**, beneath the castle, has different stonework on its upper and lower parts. This dates back to damage caused by the great floods of 1661. The floods left the south bank of the river so eroded that travellers needed to use a ladder to get on to the bridge. Before those floods the bridge had a built-in chapel where Bible clerk Cuthbert Hilton conducted numerous illegal marriages.

⑥ Turn right over the footbridge back into **Barnard Castle** and go straight ahead into **Thorngate**. Turn left along **Bridgegate**. Where the road crosses the **County Bridge** go straight on to follow a path that rounds the castle walls to the entrance. After visiting the **castle** continue past the Methodist church to the start of **Galgate**.

⑦ Turn right along **Market Street** and continue to the **Market Cross**. Carry on down **The Bank** then, at the top of **Thorngate**, go left to **Demesnes**. Retrace earlier footsteps back to the car park.

Walk 47

Wild Flowers and Moors

Walking in Baldersdale, the spartan home of Hannah Hauxwell.

•DISTANCE•	5½ miles (8.8km)
•MINIMUM TIME•	3hrs 15min
•ASCENT / GRADIENT•	750ft (229m) ▲▲ ▲
•LEVEL OF DIFFICULTY•	🚶 🚶 🚶
•PATHS•	Tracks, field and moor paths and lanes, no stiles
•LANDSCAPE•	Moor and farmland
•SUGGESTED MAP•	aqua3 OS Explorer OL31 North Pennines
•START / FINISH•	Grid reference: NY 928187
•DOG FRIENDLINESS•	Farming country, dogs should be on leads
•PARKING•	Car park by Balderhead dam
•PUBLIC TOILETS•	Near car park
•CONTRIBUTOR•	John Gillham

BACKGROUND TO THE WALK

Baldersdale is a wild and harsh upland dale with only a hint of green that surrounds the river impinging on the remote brown ridges of the Cotherstone and Hunderthwaite moors. To the west the river empties into the Tees, to the east just the rocky pork pie-like summit of Shacklesborough breaks the monochrome monotony.

Unimproved Fields

Three things brought Baldersdale to the attention of the outside world. The first was the building of the reservoirs, which brought sailors, waterskiers and anglers here; the second was the routing of the Pennine Way to these parts. The third, and perhaps the most fascinating, was a 1973 television series that detailed the life of Hannah Hauxwell. Hannah's family worked Low Birk Hat, the little farm down in the bottom of the valley by Blackton Reservoir's north west shores; the one surrounded by trees – you'll visit it later.

When Hannah's parents passed away she was left alone to work this isolated farm without the luxury of running water or electricity. She did so without the benefit of modern farming methods and without the use of artificial fertilisers. When Hannah retired in 1988 the Durham Wildlife Trust purchased her lands. They found the 'unimproved' fields of great interest with several uncommon species of plants flourishing.

The walk begins along the dam of the huge Balderhead Reservoir where you can look down the valley to the greener but pallid horizons of Teesdale. Your eyes, however will soon be transfixed to a craggy summit that ruffles the profile of Cotherstone Moor. It's known as Goldsborough and it will be the high point of the walk. It's a fine summit, one for a picnic on the rocks if the sun shines. From here you can look out across the whole of the North Pennines including the highest summit, Cross Fell.

Coming back down into the valley the route tramps the fields around Hury Reservoir, and those at the western end of Blackton Reservoir. The latter is the shallowest of the Baldersdale lakes and one fringed with wetlands. It's a haven for wildfowl here and you may see coots, moorhens, reed buntings and sedge warblers nesting: feeding visitors include the oystercatcher, snipe and redshank. During harsh winters you may spot a black grouse that has come down from the moors to feed on the birch shoots. An information board just beyond Low Birk Hat will tell you more.

The climb back to the start point involves passing Hannah's Meadow. The 17½-acre (7.1ha) nature reserve has a wide variety of grasses interspersed with colourful wild flowers like wood cranesbill, globeflower, marsh marigold, wood anemone, ragged robin and the adder's tongue fern, which only grows in meadows unpolluted by artificial fertilisers.

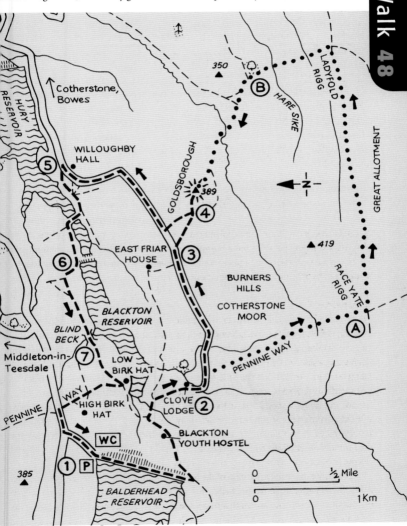

Walk 48 Directions

① Walk across the **Balderhead Dam** causeway to the south side of the reservoir. Double back left on

the stony track descending past the **Blackton Youth Hostel**. Beyond this a grass track leads down towards the **Blackton Reservoir** where it meets the **Pennine Way** track beyond a gate. It's worth detouring

Walk 48

left from here to visit the wetlands on the north west shores before returning to this point (it's also very pretty). Turn right along the track and climb past **Clove Lodge**.

② Beyond this take the tarmac lane to your left. On your left you pass the pastures of several farms, while on your right are the barren slopes of Cotherstone Moor.

③ Just beyond the driveway of **East Friar House** take the narrow path climbing half right (south east) towards the rocks of **Goldsborough** (part of the Bowes Loop Pennine Way alternative).

WHERE TO EAT AND DRINK ℹ️

The **Fox and Hounds** at Cotherstone is an 18th-century coaching inn in the village where Hannah Hauxwell retired. Very tasty meals, including vegetarian options, are available lunch times and evenings – try ratatouille-filled crêpe, baked with Cotherstone cheese. Beers include Black Sheep and John Smiths.

---

④ By the first of the rocks take the left fork to climb to the summit. Return to this position, then take a narrow right fork path that descends northwards, back to the road. Turn right along the road and follow it down to **Hury Reservoir**.

⑤ Just beyond **Willoughby Hall**, double back left along the Northumbrian Water access track, then turn right off it along the grassy causeway to the north of the reservoir. A path veers left above the north shore, climbs above the **Blackton Dam** where it goes through a gate on the right.

⑥ Through a second gate in the north-west corner of the field the path veers right alongside a line of

---

WHAT TO LOOK FOR ℹ️

You may well see the **song thrush** in or around Hannah's Meadow. Unfortunately, populations of this fine speckled-breasted member of the blackbird family are rapidly declining due to the destruction of its favoured habitats. The larger **mistle thrush** is also present. Recognise this by its slightly greyer colour and flash of white on the tail.

---

hawthorns, then turns left alongside more hawthorn trees. Past an old barn, walls to the right at first, then to the left guide the route to the footbridge across **Blind Beck**. Waymarking arrows are now aiding route-finding.

⑦ The footpath now crosses two fields, parallel with the reservoir's shoreline. In a third field, follow the dry-stone wall half-left down towards **Low Birk Hat**, then pass in front of the farmhouse to reach a stony track. The house itself is now in private ownership and it would be courteous not to pause too long here. Turn right along the gated track and climb out of the valley, past **Hannah's Meadow** and **High Birk Hat** to reach a higher road. Turn left then take the next turning on the left, a tarmac lane back to the car park.

WHILE YOU'RE THERE ℹ️

Visit **Bowes**, an historic village in the nearby Greta Valley. The Romans were here and built a fort, Lavatrae, to guard their Carlisle to York road and the approaches to the Stainmore Pass. In 1970 the fort was excavated and the archaeologists found an inscription that told of the fort's damage after a rebellion of AD 197. Much of the site has been obscured by Bowes Castle, a powerful-looking keep that is believed to have been built in the 12th century to repel raids from the Scots.

On Cotherstone Moor

Following the footsteps of the Pennine Wayfarer.
See map and information panel for Walk 48

•DISTANCE•	8½ miles (13.7km)
•MINIMUM TIME•	5hrs
•ASCENT / GRADIENT•	1,150ft (350m) ▲▲▲
•LEVEL OF DIFFICULTY•	🚶🚶🚶

Walk 49 Directions (Walk 48 option)

Goldsborough, visited on Walk 48, gives an insight into Cotherstone's lonely Pennine outposts, but this route takes you higher for longer. Here you tramp the heather and see even wider hillscapes. For much of the time you will be following the Pennine Way, both the main route and the Bowes Loop alternative.

The route leaves Walk 48 quite early. On the road above **Clove Lodge** (Point ②), ignore the first signed bridleway, but take the Pennine Way path a few paces further on. The path climbs south over the mosses of **Cotherstone Moor**, with the rounded Burners Hills to the left and the rocky knoll of Shacklesborough capping the sombre hillscape to the right. The path reaches its high point at **Race Yate Rigg** (Point Ⓐ) where there's a gate and stile at the intersection of ridge fence and ridge wall.

About 100yds (91m) or so south of this turn left through a gate to follow a bridleway westwards across **Great Allotment**. The track, sketchy at first, is always a little below the watershed. Below on your right the bleak hollow of Deep Dale leads the eye to the brighter hues of distant woodland and separates Cotherstone Moor from the darker heather moors of Ravock.

Just a few paces short of a north-south fence and gate on **Ladyfold Rigg**, leave the track for a grassy path on the left (the Bowes Loop Pennine Way alternative). Though you often suspect this faded path will disappear into the grasses it never deserts you, but weaves its way north over undulating moorland, staying close to the fence and later a wall. On the other side you'll see the warning notices of the military firing range. Note the dead pines. Some crags over that wall look inviting, and it's a shame that the figure on the top of them is no climber but a soldier!

North of **Hare Sike**, take the left of two gates (Point Ⓑ), beyond which the path veers half left across rushy moorland towards the rocky summit of **Goldsborough**. The Pennine Way path skirts the west side of the little peak, but it's a simple trackless climb to the top of the rocks (Walk 48, Point ④). From here follow the main route back down to the road and along the northern shores of the **Hury** and **Blackton reservoirs**.

Walk 50

The Bridges of Middlesbrough

A riverside figure of eight, with a train journey from Middlesbrough to Thornaby in the middle.

•DISTANCE•	6 miles (9.7km) plus 3-mile (4.8km) train journey
•MINIMUM TIME•	2hrs plus train journey
•ASCENT / GRADIENT•	Negligible ▲▲▲
•LEVEL OF DIFFICULTY•	🚶 🚶🚶 🚶🚶
•PATHS•	Riverside paths and pavements
•LANDSCAPE•	Former industrial area, riverside, fine engineering structures
•SUGGESTED MAP•	aqua3 OS Explorer 306 Middlesbrough & Hartlepool
•START / FINISH•	Grid reference: NZ 462193
•DOG FRIENDLINESS•	Can be off lead on riverside sections
•PARKING•	Tees Barrage car park, approached over Barrier from A66
•PUBLIC TOILETS•	Transporter Bridge Visitor Centre (open weekends only, but daily in school holidays) and Middlesbrough Station
•CONTRIBUTOR•	David Winpenny

Walk 50 Directions

From the **Tees Barrage** car park walk to the red-and-blue metal flags above the canoe slalom course. The Barrage was built between 1991 and 1995 and cost £54 million. It has four 50-ton gates, each 44ft (13.4m) long and 26ft (7.9m) high. The Barrage has created 11 miles (17.7km) of freshwater between Stockton and Yarm, which is used for a wide variety of leisure activities. The whitewater canoe slalom course provides exciting sport, and hosted the Canoe World Championships in 2001.

Turn right, down the slope, then left over two arched bridges. Bear right then left through the walled picnic area to join the riverside path. Turn left and follow the path, staying beside the river where the tarmac ends. Go beneath the concrete road bridge, built in 1975 to carry the A19 road. After the bridge the path becomes a track. After a metal barrier across it, go straight on towards the **Newport Bridge**, built by Dorman Long (who also built the Tyne and Sydney Harbour bridges) in 1934. The first vertical lift bridge in Britain (and the largest in the world), it was last raised in 1990 and is now permanently shut.

Climb the steps and cross the bridge. At the end of the bridge take the steps on your right and descend to the river bank, bearing right

> **WHERE TO EAT AND DRINK** ℹ️
> There is a **café** near the Tees Barrage, and a hotel and **restaurant** on the hillside above. Otherwise Middlesbrough offers a wide choice – you can reach the centre by going under the Albert Bridge before catching your train to Thornaby. Stockton also has cafés and pubs. Cross the Millennium Bridge to reach its centre.

beneath the bridge to join a tarmac track. Turn left and follow the track, keeping left where it divides. Continue along the riverside for 1½ miles (2.4km). This riverside park was once the site of the Newport Iron Works, founded in 1864. Across the river are the chemical complexes at Billingham, which opened in 1917. The river curves right. Notice the wharfs where the iron ore barges tied up to supply the ironworks.

WHILE YOU'RE THERE ⓘ

Albert Park in Linthorpe Road, Middlesbrough, is a green oasis in the town. There is a visitor centre and areas for sports and games, as well as beautifully planted flowerbeds. The refurbished Dorman Museum in the park, built after the only son of the Dorman shipbuilding family died in the Boer War, has displays of Middlesbrough history.

Near office buildings go up a grassy slope ahead and continue to a curved metal bench – there are disused slipways, where boats were once built, on the other side of the river. Turn right here and follow the path which brings you into an open area with steel sculptures of dinosaurs. This is **Teesaurus Park**, opened in 1982 on the site of a former slag heap. Keep to the left, to emerge on to a road. Turn left and follow the road, bearing left at a

roundabout, to reach a crossroads beside the **Transporter Bridge**. Symbol of Teesside, the bridge was built between 1907 and 1911, and carries 750 people and 600 vehicles across the Tees every day. The carrying car crosses in 2½ minutes, 160ft (48.7m) above the river. Turn right and follow the road to where the **Albert Bridge** takes the railway over the road. Go half right to enter the railway station via a subway.

Take the train one stop to **Thornaby**. Leave Thornaby Station over the footbridge and go straight ahead over the grassed area, bearing left at the end to a roundabout. Turn right, following the Stockton Town Centre footway signs. If you look to the left you will see a replica of Captain Cook's ship *Endeavour*, and the **Teesquay Millennium Bridge**, opened in December 2000. Go over a small bridge, then bear right then left to reach another roundabout. Go straight ahead over the **Princess of Wales Bridge**.

At the end bear right to join a track going towards the river. Go left through a narrow gateway into woodland, then continue along the riverside as far as the **Tees Barrage**. Go underneath it and bear left to pass the canoe slalom and return to the red-and-blue metal flags.

WHAT TO LOOK FOR ⓘ

The area around the Transporter Bridge has largely been cleared of the tightly-packed **houses** that once accommodated the thousands who toiled in the ironworks, but some still remain. Middlesbrough grew from a population of just 25 in 1801 to 91,000 a century later. It was called 'youngest child of England's enterprise, the infant Hercules'. Many of the houses the workers lived in were hard up against the ironworks, and their lives were dominated by smoke, dirt, heat and noise. Two-bedroomed houses could hold as many as 20 people, who slept and worked in shifts, so the beds were never cold. The women were condemned to a life of drudgery, trying to keep families together and prevent illness. It is not surprising that the children, taken from this squalor to church-organised picnics on the edge of the North York Moors, believed they were in heaven.

Walking in Safety

All these walks are suitable for any reasonably fit person, but less experienced walkers should try the easier walks first. Route finding is usually straightforward, but you will find that an Ordnance Survey map is a useful addition to the route maps and descriptions.

Risks

Although each walk here has been researched with a view to minimising the risks to the walkers who follow its route, no walk in the countryside can be considered to be completely free from risk. Walking in the outdoors will always require a degree of common sense and judgement to ensure that it is as safe as possible.

- Be particularly careful on cliff paths and in upland terrain, where the consequences of a slip can be very serious.

- Remember to check tidal conditions before walking on the seashore.

- Some sections of route are by, or cross, busy roads. Take care and remember traffic is a danger even on minor country lanes.

- Be careful around farmyard machinery and livestock, especially if you have children with you.

- Be aware of the consequences of changes in the weather and check the forecast before you set out. Carry spare clothing and a torch if you are walking in the winter months. Remember the weather can change very quickly at any time of the year, and in moorland and heathland areas, mist and fog can make route finding much harder. Don't set out in these conditions unless you are confident of your navigation skills in poor visibility. In summer remember to take account of the heat and sun; wear a hat and carry spare water.

- On walks away from centres of population you should carry a whistle and survival bag. If you do have an accident requiring the emergency services, make a note of your position as accurately as possible and dial 999.

Acknowledgements

Dennis Kelsall thanks the staffs of the Rights of Way section at the Northumberland County Council, Northumberland Wildlife Trust and English Heritage as well as staff at the tourist information offices in both Berwick and Morpeth.

AQUA3 AA Publishing and Outcrop Publishing Services would like to thank Chartech for supplying aqua3 maps for this book.
For more information visit their website: www.aqua3.com.

Series management: Outcrop Publishing Services Limited, Cumbria
Series editor: Chris Bagshaw **Copy editor:** Pam Stagg
Front cover: www.BritainonView.com **Back cover:** AA Photo Library/J Martin